C000061976

International and Development Education

Series Editors
John N. Hawkins
Asia Pacific Higher Education Research Partnership
University of California, Los Angeles
Los Angeles, CA, USA

W. James Jacob
University of Memphis
Memphis, TN, USA

The International and Development Education series focuses on the complementary areas of comparative, international, and development education. Books emphasize a number of topics ranging from key international education issues, trends, and reforms to examinations of national education systems, social theories, and development education initiatives. Local, national, regional, and global volumes (single authored and edited collections) constitute the breadth of the series and offer potential contributors a great deal of latitude based on interests and cutting-edge research.

International Editorial Advisory Board
Clementina Acedo, *Webster University, Switzerland*
Philip G. Altbach, *Boston University, USA*
Carlos E. Blanco, *Universidad Central de Venezuela*
Oswell C. Chakulimba, *University of Zambia*
Sheng Yao Cheng, *National Chung Cheng University, Taiwan*
Edith Gnanadass, *University of Memphis, USA*
Wendy Griswold, *University of Memphis, USA*
Ruth Hayhoe, *University of Toronto, Canada*
Yuto Kitamura, *Tokyo University, Japan*
Wanhua Ma, *Peking University, China*
Donna Menke, *University of Memphis, USA*
Ka Ho Mok, *Lingnan University, China*
Christine Musselin, *Sciences Po, France*
Deane E. Neubauer, *University of Hawaii and East-West Center, USA*
Yusuf K. Nsubuga, *Ministry of Education and Sports, Uganda*
Namgi Park, *Gwangju National University of Education, Republic of Korea*
Val D. Rust, *University of California, Los Angeles, USA*
Suparno, *State University of Malang, Indonesia*
John C. Weidman, *University of Pittsburgh, USA*
Husam Zaman, *UNESCO/Regional Center of Quality and Excellence in Education, Saudi Arabia*

More information about this series at
http://www.palgrave.com/gp/series/14849

Deane E. Neubauer · Ka Ho Mok ·
Sachi Edwards
Editors

Contesting
Globalization and
Internationalization
of Higher Education

Discourse and Responses in the Asia Pacific Region

Editors
Deane E. Neubauer
Asia Pacific Higher Education
Research Partnership
East–West Center
Honolulu, HI, USA

Ka Ho Mok
Lingnan University
Hong Kong, China

Sachi Edwards
Graduate School of Education
The University of Tokyo
Tokyo, Japan

International and Development Education
ISBN 978-3-030-26229-7   ISBN 978-3-030-26230-3   (eBook)
https://doi.org/10.1007/978-3-030-26230-3

© The Editor(s) (if applicable) and The Author(s), under exclusive license to Springer
Nature Switzerland AG 2019
This work is subject to copyright. All rights are solely and exclusively licensed by the
Publisher, whether the whole or part of the material is concerned, specifically the rights
of translation, reprinting, reuse of illustrations, recitation, broadcasting, reproduction
on microfilms or in any other physical way, and transmission or information storage and
retrieval, electronic adaptation, computer software, or by similar or dissimilar methodology
now known or hereafter developed.
The use of general descriptive names, registered names, trademarks, service marks, etc. in this
publication does not imply, even in the absence of a specific statement, that such names are
exempt from the relevant protective laws and regulations and therefore free for general use.
The publisher, the authors and the editors are safe to assume that the advice and
information in this book are believed to be true and accurate at the date of publication.
Neither the publisher nor the authors or the editors give a warranty, expressed or implied,
with respect to the material contained herein or for any errors or omissions that may have
been made. The publisher remains neutral with regard to jurisdictional claims in published
maps and institutional affiliations.

Cover illustration: © MirageC/Moment/gettyimages

This Palgrave Macmillan imprint is published by the registered company Springer Nature
Switzerland AG
The registered company address is: Gewerbestrasse 11, 6330 Cham, Switzerland

*This volume is dedicated to our friend and colleague
Professor John W. Harkins who has served over the years
as a mentor to many in the field of higher education.*

CONTENTS

EDITORS AND CONTRIBUTORS

About the Editors

Deane E. Neubauer is Professor Emeritus of Political Science at the University of Hawaii, Manoa. He currently also serves as the Associate Director of the Asia Pacific Higher Education Research Partnership (APHERP) which conducts a wide range of policy-focused research with a special focus on higher education. He is also currently an adjunct fellow of the East-West Center, in Honolulu, Hawaii. Over the course of his career, he has focused on a variety of political and policy areas including democratic theory, public policy, elections, and various policy foci, including education, health, agriculture, and communication. He has held a wide variety of administrative positions at the University of Hawaii, Manoa, and the 10 campus University of Hawaii system.

Ka Ho Mok is Vice-President and Lam Man Tsan Chair Professor of Comparative Policy at Lingnan University, Hong Kong.

Sachi Edwards is a JSPS Post-Doctoral Research Fellow in the Graduate School of Education at the University of Tokyo, Japan. She has a Ph.D. in Higher Education, Student Affairs, and International Education Policy from the University of Maryland. Her research focuses on analyzing policies and pedagogies that promote increased understanding and appreciation of diverse worldviews at various levels (local, national, international). She is the co-editor of the book series, *Spirituality, Religion,* *and Education* (Palgrave Macmillan). Two of her recent publications include *Critical Conversations About Religion* (2016) and *Contemplative Pedagogies in K-12, University, and Community Settings* (co-edited, forthcoming), both with Information Age Publishing.

Contributors

Antonio Bolanos Casanova Jr. is a Ph.D. student in the International Doctoral Program in Asia-Pacific Studies at the National Chengchi University in Taipei City, Taiwan. His research interests include culture "immigration" and international education in the Asia Pacific Region.

(Kent) Sheng Yao Cheng is current Director of the Graduate Institute of Education at National Chung Cheng University in Taiwan. Professor Cheng got his Ph.D. degree at UCLA in 2004 and his recent research interests are disadvantaged students and remedial teaching, higher education, teacher education, comparative education, and sociology of education. Professor Cheng also serves as the Editor in Chief, Taiwan *Journal of Sociology of Education*, the Director of Institute for Disadvantaged Students' Learning at Yonglin Hope School between 2009 and 2017, the Board Member of Chinese Comparative Education Society-Taipei and Taiwan Association of Sociology of Education, Program Chair of Comparative and International Education Society (CIES) SIG: Higher Education (2009–2013), International Advisor of the National Center for University Entrance Examinations in Japan since the year of 2009, Affiliated Faculty in the Institute of International Studies in Education at University of Pittsburgh since the year of 2008, and Fulbright Visiting Scholar at University of Pittsburgh in 2011–2012. Professor Cheng has published dozens of journal articles and book chapters both in Chinese and English. He is also the editor of *Indigenous Education: Language, Culture, and Identity* published by Springer in 2015.

Chuing Prudence Chou is a Professor of Education at National Chengchi University. She received a Ph.D. in Comparative and International Education from the University of California in Los Angeles in 1992. Her teaching efforts focus on comparative education, classroom management, special education issues in the People's Republic of China, gender equity education, and other special topics pertaining to higher education. She has worked in the fields of higher education, social service, and women's studies and has written and edited numerous books, articles, reports, and papers. Her recent research has focused on the broad context of American Doctoral training of China specialists, addressing the ways in which young generations of China experts interpret the role of their US-based doctoral training on their lives—both personally and socially—as well as the impact, as US-trained experts, these individuals have had on China studies in China, Taiwan, and the USA.

Futao Huang is Professor at the Research Institute for Higher Education, Hiroshima University, Japan. Before he came to Japan in 1999, he taught and conducted research in several Chinese universities. His research interests include internationalization of higher education, the academic profession, and higher education in East Asia. He has published widely in Chinese, English, and Japanese languages. He is the editor of *Higher Education Forum* and the member of Advisory Editorial Boards of *Higher Education, Journal of Studies in International Education*, and *International Journal of Educational Development*, etc. Currently, he is also a Guest Professor of Shanghai Jiao Tong University and Adjunct Professor of Zhejiang University, China.

Yue Kan is Professor and Deputy Dean of College of Education, Zhejiang University China. He received his Ph.D. at Zhejiang University of China and then was a postdoctoral fellow at Beijing Normal University, China. He was a visiting scholar at Institute of Education (IOE), University of London and Graduate School of Education and Information Studies (GSE&IS), and University of California, Los Angeles (UCLA). He specialized in the comparative study of educational policy, and his current research interests focus on the international organizations and global governance in education, and accountability in higher education. He is also a member of Comparative and International Education Society (CIES) and Board of Chinese Comparative Education Society (CCES).

Yuyang Kang is Ph.D. candidate in Sociology and Social Policy at Lingnan University. Before joining Lingnan, she studied at King's College London and Jinan University. Her research interests are in the subfield of internationalization of higher education, student migration, and local innovation development. Her current projects focus on changing university–industry–government networks in knowledge transfer in

Hong Kong and Shenzhen. Her Ph.D. is funded by Hong Kong Ph.D. Fellowship and she is also the awardee of Sino-British Fellowship Trust Fund and Fung Scholarship.

Yuto Kitamura is an Associate Professor at Graduate School of Education, The University of Tokyo. He received Ph.D. in Education from the University of California, Los Angeles (UCLA). He has been mainly conducting his research on education policy in developing countries in Southeast Asia, particularly Cambodia. His recent publications include *The Political Economy of Schooling in Cambodia: Issues of Quality and Equity* (co-edited, Palgrave Macmillan, 2016) and *Japanese Education in a Global Age: Sociological Reflections and Future Directions* (co-edited, Springer, 2018).

Shangbo Li (Ph.D., Tokyo University of Foreign Studies, 2004) is a Professor at the University of International Business and Economics of China in Beijing and Specially Approved Research Fellow at J. F. Oberlin University in Tokyo. She has been a visiting scholar at the East–West Center (2010–2011). She specializes in Higher Education and Japanese Studies.

John Lowe is an Associate Professor in the School of Education at the University of Nottingham, Ningbo, China. He has occupied various roles in education over the last 45 years and in more than 20 countries worldwide. For some years now, his primary research interest has been in the relationships between education and social change—which is one of the reasons he recently chose to work in China—and his research most recently has focused on aspects of higher education and universities. He has particular concerns, on both professional and ideological grounds, over the directions in which many contemporary higher education systems and institutions appear to be being led.

Sudakarn Patamadilok has been a Lecturer of English, a trainer of teachers, and a freelance translator in the TESOL context for more than 20 years and currently serves as Deputy Dean for International Relations and Student Affairs at Kasetsart University, Bangkok, Thailand. As an experienced administrator in educational institutes, Sudakarn realizes how top-down policy has an impact on academic instruction. Her main interest is to find a platform built through efforts such as curriculum reform, student/staff exchange, and training courses, among other practices, all of which benefit students, teachers, researchers, employees, and all people in society and on earth.

Bingna Xu is a Ph.D. candidate at College of Education, Zhejiang University, China. Her research focuses on the internalization of higher education and educational issues related to the Belt and Road Initiative (BRI).

Rui Yang is Professor and Associate Dean (cross-border and international engagement) in the Faculty of Education at The University of Hong Kong. With over two and a half decades of academic career in China, Australia, and Hong Kong, he has an impressive track record on research at the interface of Chinese and Western traditions in education. He has established his reputation among scholars in English and Chinese national languages in the fields of comparative and international education and Chinese higher education. His international reputation is evidenced by his extensive list of publications, research projects, invited keynote lectures in international and regional conferences, leadership in professional associations, and membership in editorial boards of scholarly journals. Bridging the theoretical thrust of comparative education and the applied nature of international education, his research interests include education policy sociology, comparative and cross-cultural studies in education, international higher education, educational development in Chinese societies, and international politics in educational research.

Minho Yeom is Professor of the Department of Education in the College of Education, Chonnam National University, Gwangju, South Korea, where he once served as Director of the Center for Teaching and Learning. He has written widely on issues of higher education reform at the micro- and macro-levels, particularly curriculum changes, learning communities, writing center operation, and faculty professional development as well as government policy. He holds a Ph.D. in Educational Administration and Policy from the University of Pittsburgh, USA. His major research interests include educational policy development and evaluation, higher education reform, comparative international education, teacher education, and writing across the curriculum.

LIST OF FIGURES

LIST OF TABLES

CHAPTER 1

Introduction: Contesting Globalization and Its Discourses

Deane E. Neubauer and Sachi Edwards

The chapters in this volume derive from a research seminar hosted by the Asia Pacific Higher Education Research Partnership (APHERP) at Lingnan University in Hong Kong in November 2017. The invited participants were asked to reflect on the emergence to that point in time of "a keen and renewed interest in the rise of nationalism (and sometimes nationalism within regionalism) within the complex patterns of what has been commonly termed 'contemporary globalization.'" Within that frame of reference, they were asked to reflect further on the implications for such

D. E. Neubauer (✉)
Asia Pacific Higher Education Research Partnership,
East–West Center, Honolulu, HI, USA
e-mail: deanen@hawaii.edu

University of Hawaii at Manoa, Honolulu, HI, USA

S. Edwards
Graduate School of Education,
The University of Tokyo, Bunkyo, Tokyo, Japan
e-mail: ste@hawaii.edu

© The Author(s) 2019   1
D. E. Neubauer et al. (eds.), *Contesting Globalization and Internationalization of Higher Education*,
International and Development Education,
https://doi.org/10.1007/978-3-030-26230-3_1

on the status of higher education (HE) within the Asia Pacific region. The participants were, for the most part, drawn from the institutions that were members of APHERP, which, in turn, was a membership organization drawn largely from associations developed by the East–West Center in Honolulu, Hawai'i. APHERP and its predecessor organization the International Forum for Education 2020 (IFE 2020) had been sponsoring a series of research seminars since 2004 focused on the many ways HE was developing within the region as part of the growing and expanding the reality of global interdependence. The more recent rise of various forms of nationalism was clearly, in many ways, a significant departure from what has become increasingly accepted as the dominant modality of much of international HE. It also seemed to be highly dynamic in both kind and reach, despite its relatively recent emergence. This volume explores multiple aspects of this nationalist phenomenon into the early months of 2018, moving back and forth from consideration of the broader dynamics of international engagement embedded within globalization to those more recently introduced and privileged by these nationalist impulses that are resulting in a re-problematizing of "the international."

The Chapter 2 by John Lowe and Neubauer explores two "modal" responses to the recent nationalist resurgence as it impacts HE. One, both sensible and limited in its perspective and range, is the response by HE professionals about their "very livelihoods themselves." The future of HE as an institutional embodiment of contemporary nations has arisen over the past three or so decades within a very definite international and global context, as the annual movement of international students throughout the world approaches two million. Thus, many HE professionals are concerned about how national systems will be impacted if such elements of nationalism operate to erode this massive student flow. The other response, which the authors characterize as "the intellectual response," arises as scholars across many disciplines and nations seek to understand the implications the nationalist resurgence has on the extent and nature of multiple discourses. Part of their reaction is an effort to "place these events within understandable, and optimally critical, frameworks that allow further explication, analysis and understanding to take place." Within this framework, the authors address various efforts to redefine and explore basic concepts that have flowed through the previously widely accepted international context itself.

In the following chapter, Minho Yeom reprises the development of international HE in the South Korean context over the past several decades. In so doing, he presents four differing development theories—modernization theory, subordinate theory, semi-peripheral theory, and social mobility theory—each of which has had some significant "purchase" within a South Korean context. He then explores their differential relevance through the use of statistical data organized around four indicators of internationalism in Korean HE: the number of Korean overseas students studying over the past four years; their distribution by country of destination; the number of international students studying at domestic institutions; and the influence of the English language in lectures and research in Korean higher education institutions (HEI). Yeom seeks to locate these major characteristics of Korean HE within the four development theories he has chosen to explore.

In Chapter 4, Rui Yang details the extensive efforts being made throughout parts of Asia, and specifically in Hong Kong, to develop HEIs that have engaged contemporary globalization and internationalization by integrating European and North American cultural traditions with authentic Confucian sociocultural contexts. Over the past decade or so, he argues, East Asian countries have placed such cultural integration high on their institutional agendas and have, overall, achieved considerable progress. This policy stance has opened spaces for East Asian universities both to contest the historical dominance of Western HEIs and to offer HE experiences to students that are significantly different from those available outside the region. Within the framework of this volume, Yang's findings underscore the degree to which some intellectual centers have sought to negotiate a path between nationalism and globalization, rather than adopting a contested engagement, by framing their own intellectual endeavors with multiple cultural and intellectual traditions.

The following chapter by Yue Kan and Bingna Xu posits yet another alternative to the dichotomy between globalization and nationalism that, in their view, resides in China's Belt and Road Initiative (BRI). Their presentation elaborates on how this initiative "could be…a solution to mediate the conflicts between nationalism and globalization" and suggests implications for HE development across a range of countries that, to some extent, have been excluded or marginalized in the overall context of the internationalization of HE. Focusing initially on the seemingly endemic inequalities of development that over three decades of globalization have produced, the authors raise two basic questions that lie at the crux of the dichotomy that has emerged: One, what is the role (and one presumes here by extension—"the legitimate role"—of nationalism in globalization? And second: Does "stepping back" from the world, as implicit within the notions of Brexit and "Trumpian nationalism" really benefit countries? Their exploration of the BRI is an effort to begin a useful discussion of such issues.

In Chapter 6, Kent Chang documents the unique case of Taiwan as it has sought to develop a competitive HE system both within the shadow of its much larger and better established regional "neighbors" and in the face of what has become a defining demographic shift within the country. Within the span of three decades, the country was faced with initial demands to radically expand its HE system to meet domestic demand and to facilitate the needs of a rapidly expanding industrial sector, followed closely by the onset of the demographic crisis of a rapidly declining birth rate. This has dovetailed into placing Taiwan in a competitive context in which it has been forced to increase both the reach and quality of its HEIs. Chang borrows two related concepts from the American education experience, the *Race to the Top* and *Back to Basics* to characterize the range of policies and programs developed by the Taiwan government to meet these urgent HE needs within an increasingly competitive international/global environment. In doing so, he highlights the tensions between what he labels as the impact factor and the social impact factor of HE reforms in Taiwan.

In the following chapter, Shangbo Li guides the reader through the extensive provision of HE policies initiated in Japan by the Ministry of Education, Culture, Sports, Science and Technology (MEXT) as it has sought, over the past two decades, to guide Japanese HE through the complex transition from a highly nationalized system to one increasingly geared toward preparing students for a highly globalized world and also providing Japanese industry and culture with the capacities for faring successfully in international competition. One aspect of the Japan system of HE (discernable in some others as well) has been its high degree of state centralization, which operates not only to directly create change within the core system of publically supported HEIs, but also to provide a compelling "surrounding environment" for the much larger system of private HE. Here, Li is suggesting that within this particular Japan context, the presumptive tension between nationalism and globalization is, in large part, resolved by the essential fact that in such a highly centralized system, national policy determines its role within the broader global environment.

Futao Huang follows this framing of Japan HE in Chapter 8 with a review of its progress since the ending of World War II and the focused role that central government ministries have had on both its initial post-war framing and subsequent developments. Of particular interest is the influence exercised over the whole of the Japanese HE system by the various forces of internationalism that came to operate within it as it matured in the decades after the war, a period in which explicit efforts to engage Western values were made to replace the imperialistic and nationalist emphases that had characterized Japan HE in the pre-war period. To provide a view of the more contemporary period, he gives particular attention to two large-scale surveys focused on the more recent period (2008 and 2017) with reporting provided by university administrators who provide their combined assessments of the extent of Japan HE internationalization across a variety of fields of endeavor.

In Chapter 9, Chuing Prudence Cho and Antonio Bolanos Casanova Jr. return us to Taiwan with a different perspective on the common theme of Chapter 6—Taiwan's higher education pursuit of "World Class Status." Their critique of the current system and its policy dynamics focuses on the various "disciplines and distortions" that can and do result when governments with a major investment in HE adopt a commitment to an assessment modality that is nested within the current system of global rankings. Useful for some purposes, such systems are inherently reductionist and driven to simplify significant features of the HE endeavor to those which can be or have been made to be quantifiable. As the authors put it, these features "often come with unintended consequences, at the expense of the overall academic endeavor." Their analysis proceeds to focus on how the dual pursuits of "global excellence" and "local equity" can result in what they regard as "an obsessive pursuit of 'world-class status.'"

Chapter 10 shifts our focus to Thailand where Sudakarn Patamadilok takes on the challenges that increasing nationalism poses to internationalism at the HE level by focusing on the efforts of Thai universities (in general and in specific, her own, Naresuan University) to navigate the tensions between these two powerful global forces. After a review of the general global HE environment, she provides a case study of Naresuan University in the context of what has been labeled the "5 Higher Education Shields" designed to sustain and protect the essence of Naresuan University "from the possible negative effects of seeking to transition to meet the demands of global standards and relevance too quickly." The five shields are: curriculum reform; student/staff exchange; the creation of relevant training courses; developing international themes and models within a range of classroom performances, including drama; and research endeavors including those that require postgraduate students to provide their theses in English. In recognizing that many of these activities are also present in other universities, she emphasizes that within the Naresuan context, they serve "not only

[to] prevent the hazardous clash of nationalism and internationalism, but also promote understanding and harmony for the two polarities through learning, working and doing activities among both Thai and foreign students and staff."

In Chapter 11, Sachi Edwards and Yuto Kitamura discuss the phenomenon of the rapidly increasing mobility of students and researchers that is emblematic of the internationalization of HE. They explore the soft power reasoning that, to this point, dominates policy discourse on the issue, and present a new angle of analysis by applying the lenses of "knowledge diplomacy" and "worldview diversity education." According to the authors, HE, as an institution, has both the potential and the responsibility, through internationalization efforts, to "promote understanding of differences in worldview and to temper the recent resurgence of nationalism and xenophobia we are witnessing across the globe." While their analysis is general in nature and intended for a broad-reaching conversation about approaches to HE internationalization (generally) and student/researcher mobility initiatives (specifically), they offer examples from Japan and the United States to demonstrate the kind of initiatives they see as responses to HE internationalization and globalization that prioritize knowledge sharing and an appreciation of diverse worldviews.

The concluding substantive contribution by Yuyang Kang investigates the rise of international branch campuses in China, of which, by 2016, there were six, enrolling over 6000 Chinese students. In her treatment of these institutions, Kang emphasizes the role of institutional social capital and how it influences the lives of these Chinese students, especially within the context of increasing nationalism. She concludes that even with the curtailment of some aspects of institutional social capital taking place within the rising climate of nationalism, students continue to have significant opportunities to explore and expand their social capital within the broadened cultural capital of the international branch campus. Drawing on her qualitative research, Kang finds that many students have certain expectations for the benefits to be gained through the acquisition of social capital afforded by attending an international branch campus, but that, in practice, securing a job postgraduation is not one of those benefits.

In our conclusion, we seek to weigh the findings of the studies reported on in this volume in the context of the continued pattern of actions across the global that have added to, and in some important respects changed, the global climate of increasing nationalism as it has affected higher education in the Asia Pacific region.

CHAPTER 2

Internationalization, Globalization and Institutional Roles in the Face of Rising Nationalisms

John Lowe and Deane E. Neubauer

INTRODUCTION

For many years now, numerous countries, institutions, and individuals have invested in a commitment to the internationalization of higher education (HE), whether for economic/financial, political/ideological, or academic/intellectual reasons. More recently, those of us who have been so committed have felt a rising concern—one might even say a 'fear'—

J. Lowe (✉)
University of Nottingham, Ningbo, China
e-mail: John.Lowe@nottingham.edu.cn

D. E. Neubauer
Asia Pacific Higher Education Research Partnership,
East–West Center, Honolulu, HI, USA
e-mail: deanen@hawaii.edu

University of Hawaii at Manoa, Honolulu, HI, USA

© The Author(s) 2019
D. E. Neubauer et al. (eds.), *Contesting Globalization and Internationalization of Higher Education*,
International and Development Education,
https://doi.org/10.1007/978-3-030-26230-3_2

7

over the appearance and strengthening of various forms and expressions of nationalism that run counter to the ideals and aspirations that commonly informed our commitment. Examples are legion and globally dispersed, but the 'Brexit' withdrawal of the United Kingdom from the European Union and decisions by the Trump administrations to bar access to American institutions for individuals from specified Muslim countries are perhaps particularly pertinent for higher education, given the major role those two countries play in HE internationalization, notably in the international flows of students and academics. These nationalist trends have often fed on and been complemented by negative reactions in many countries—most recently and spectacularly the USA and parts of Europe—to upticks in migration triggered by those fleeing unwanted and unsafe conditions in their own countries, and (again with the USA as exemplar) a focused hostility toward issues embedded within international trade. Leading scholars of international HE, Philip Altbach and Hans de Wit, have expressed these fears of a threat to HE internationalization in various papers. In 2015, they noted the challenge posed by increased 'nationalist, religious and ideological conflicts' to 'the original ideas international cooperation and exchange in higher education' (p. 5), while in 2017 they graphically drew on Marx's terminology of a stalking 'spectre,' this time taking the form of 'xenophobic nationalism' haunting international higher education. They have repeatedly expressed the fear that many of us must feel that these nationalist movements could put an end to HE internationalism or at a lesser remove limit or distort the international options available within the broader HE community, coming as they do in what many had previously viewed as a significant and sustainable trajectory toward a creative and transformative period in the overall history of HE, but which must now undergo major 'rethinking' (Altbach and de Wit 2015, 2017, 2018).

Within the academic community, and particularly those parts of this community which have been most deeply committed to an internationalist perspective in HE, two modal responses have emerged from this apparent contest of views and orientations. One has been an all-too understandable—if limited—concern by individuals and by institutions as a whole for their very livelihoods and continued existence—a phenomenon that can present itself as yet another form of academic retrenchment. This could be presented as a pragmatic or 'realist' position that accepts the changing global context and the limited real power afforded to HE institutions and then seeks to 'make the best of it' in order to preserve institutional core business, where 'business' is the key word. The other response might be characterized as 'the intellectual response,' a quite typical (and many would regard fitting) effort to place these events within understandable, and optimally critical, frameworks that allow further explication, analysis, and understanding to take place. Interestingly, we might present this as the 'traditional'—and, therefore, more conservative—position on the social role of HE institutions and their academic staff. Expressed in this way, the two positions appear as manifestations of a wider contest over the role and purpose of HE within contemporary society.

At this point, it is important to make a distinction between national state involvement in the direction and regulation of HE and the current rise of 'nationalism' as a state political and cultural orientation. Usher (2017) points out how, historically, universities have been co-opted into the project of building nation-states, a process he contrasts with an even earlier, perhaps over-idealized, age of university autonomy. In view of the parallels we draw below between aspects of the current state of the world and those pertaining in the late nineteenth century, it is interesting that Usher uses the emergence of a unified Germany in that era as a paradigmatic example of this linkage between HE development and nation-state construction concludes that: 'The research university is thus *at best* an instrument of the nation-state, and more often than not one of nationalism as well' (Usher, p. 1). We would argue that, as his analysis actually suggests, this relationship is historically contingent. The observation that the current rise in support for nationalist-populist political movements is often explained as a 'reaction' to preceding trends of globalization-internationalism reveals that positioning options remain contested and open.

The pitting of these seemingly polar positions may lead to an eventual 'settlement' of the contest with one side winning and the other losing, or at least a shift in the balance of institutional power between them. Various outcomes may be predicted, dependent on the particular balance achieved, leading to an overall reconstituting of many aspects of the HE community, or its fragmentation, that in the end could cost many their livelihoods. This concern appears to exist in observable contexts in which participants seek first and foremost to frame, describe, and analyze this 'confrontation' in terms of its intellectual dimensions and consequences (Usher 2017). Assuming the putative accuracy of framing this contest as such—that is, as 'separable positions'—appears to be a distressing situation in and of itself. However, the effort proceeds, 'sorting out' this seeming confrontation between nationalism and internationalism as it is emerging within HE contexts, increasingly appears to be a continuing task for the whole of the HE community, both broadly and narrowly conceived.

Reprising 'International'

Conventional notions of 'international' as both a noun and adjective have a comfortable and familiar sense to them, ready partners as it were within everyday and even academic 'speech.' But, with a bit of closer inspection, one finds a distressing and repeated ambiguity to notions of the international. To take just two examples, Theresa May, the British Prime Minister, has described Britain as being 'profoundly internationalist' in spite of the widely held perception to the contrary signified by Britain's withdrawal from Brexit (World Economic Forum 2017). Another familiar usage comes from the influential work of Jane Knight (2004, p. 11) in which she defines HE internationalization in terms of introducing 'the international, the multicultural, or the global' into all aspects of university life. What, we might ask ourselves, could be 'wrong' with that? We ask the reader to think about a range of events, or organizations, or literally anything accepted within common usage as 'international' and ask whether these diverse events or contexts share a common meaning—and if so, what is it?

We approach an 'answer' to our own query by exploring the emergence and usage of notions of internationalization and globalization and the multiple meanings they have acquired in diverse usage over an extended period of time. What are the implications for our understanding of the current intersect between these two important 'global forces,' for example, when placed in the complex contexts as developed differentially by Rowe (2005), Ferguson (2009), or Gills (2001), which point to a distinctive former era of globalization, namely that at the beginning of the nineteenth century and well into the following twentieth (or in Gills case, well before that!). Within these earlier contexts, one would find eras of booming international trade, overall with almost as large a contribution to their own GDP as the current one. Within the nineteenth century period, in particular we find the societies of major global actors being driven by new technologies which (among other things) allowed for a much greater mobility of goods, finance (including foreign direct investment—FDI), and people—proportionately an even greater proportion of the global population than currently. Searching a bit further, we would find that the core belief system having come into vogue in the nineteenth-century occurrence was that of economic/political liberalism. Overall, people and countries were collectively motivated by the theory that international trade led to international interdependence, which in turn led to international order, which led to peace.

So, we would ask ourselves: What happened? The answer, of course, is that two world wars happened, separated by a massive economic depression—so massive in fact that it would go down in modern world history as 'The Great Depression.' To gain some perspective on the current usages and views of internationalism, it is mindful to ask ourselves: Where did the theory go wrong?

One useful place to start is with two well-known scholars of globalization, David Rowe (2005) and Joseph E. Stiglitz (2016). Within these two powerful depictions of the current era, we find a repeated tale of identity loss/threat, feelings of disempowerment, and a loss of status and self-esteem—much the 'social cocktail' that many contemporary scholars find fueling the 'Trump phenomenon' (Williams 2017) and other 'anti-liberal' social responses in various countries.[1] Accompanying these 'outcries,' directed at what is widely perceived as 'excessive internationalism,' we observe in many countries, most specifically those commonly viewed at the forefront of contemporary globalization, a desire to return to a putative national 'golden age,' e.g., *Make America Great Again!*, restore traditional British values, the China dream—in short—echoes of the past in the present.

Having digested all of the foregoing, one might still want to ask: What does all of this have to do with 'international'? One response is that the current emphasis on 'international' is a form of response to globalization, in whatever manner people perceive it, but often with a sense that as a process, it in some way 'stands above' nations and what they have come to mean—most importantly to those who look to that identification. Globalization in this view is often viewed as outside conventional and accepted notions of restraint and character—a term that for many calls forth a process that is proceeding recklessly and without measure or control. Or, framed somewhat differently, one can suggest that the ideological drivers of globalization in turn also influence the ideological interpretations of the international or internationalization. We may wish to ask in this regard after some notion of historical continuity: Are these notions and attributes of the international essentially what they also meant in the late nineteenth and early twentieth centuries? What, let us ask, were some of the less fortunate connotations of internationalism in that period, to wit: national hubris, cultural arrogance, racist hierarchies, the 'white man's burden,' colonialism...economic liberalism? What, we may ask again, has been bundled together into this hodge-podge of meanings and implications to which we may have indiscriminately added such 'vectored' terms as neoliberalism, markets, and even democracy itself. The essential issue in all of this conjecture is what we mean and can mean by the language we use in our contemporary contexts and what can and does this imply both for how we seek conceptual clarification within HE contexts and where universities come to play a significant and defensible role in this overall tangle of discourse(s).

Here, we can raise a small, but important set of questions about the varied and emerging roles of HE. First maybe the range of implications touched off by prevailing notions of mass versus elite education. On the one hand, any number of commentators have opined on both the value and implications of this development, especially when placed (as it perhaps most often is) within the context of viewing the massification of HE as being essential to broadening the democratic capacities of societies, but also as essential to maintaining a current and competitive posture as a nation within the realities of emergent, technologically driven societies. Indeed, in what is perceived as an increasingly permeable global market for talent, some such as Michaels et al. (2001) have gone so far as to see this as a 'global war for talent'—with the inescapable implication that a nation either competes effectively in such a context or loses. Universities, as key producers of both human 'talent' and 'marketable' new knowledge, have found themselves recruited into this 'war.' This induction has been made easier to the point of inevitability by a series of changes in HE policy and management environments that includes: massification more-or-less forcing the need for user fees where they did not exist before, and the subsequent emergence of students as 'customers'; increased reliance on government funding and hence direction for research; closer links with business and industry and the commodification of 'intellectual property'; and the growth of 'new managerialism' in university governance, borrowed from the corporate world and with its culture and practices of 'accountability,' performance targets, and other increasingly bureaucratic control paraphernalia. Binding much of these trends together is that set of ideologies and practices covered by the all-embracing but difficult to define term 'neoliberalism' (Ball 2015, for example, but accounts are legion). In fitting with the influence of neoliberalism, the roles of the university have been relentlessly and not always so gradually modified. HE has increasingly come to be valued as a private rather than a public good, as a tool to enhance individual economic positioning through enhancing personal 'employability.' Collini opines that as a result of these and other changes, the universities of Britain 'are now principally centres of scientific and technological research and, increasingly, of vocational and professional training' (2012, pp. 30–31). Although the United Kingdom might be seen as more willingly embracing neoliberalism than many other countries, these trends in HE are to be observed in many national systems.

Is it the case, we need to ask again, whether the current rationales and/or drivers of the current attitudes toward and practices in the internationalization of HE lie within these frameworks? If so, one might argue, much of what we do as academics has come to fall within the intent of providing HE graduates with the international communication skills perceived to be required for enhanced employability. Or...to suggest even more instrumental purposes served by these HE processes, is the move toward 'the international' currently fueled primarily by the need to recruit such students to meet financial shortfalls, to fill gaps in local skills provision, or to enhance global esteem and/or even as a means of projecting 'soft power'? Once again, all of these goals are readily identifiable in national systems and institutions, although some emphasized more than others in different contexts.

Within this complex and perhaps equally confused setting, it is appropriate in our view to raise the primary question of what the possibilities are for HE in what has become this highly instrumentalized context. Certainly, one response, admittedly conservative given the context outlined above, is to reaffirm the university's commitment to its traditional 'core business.' In our view, this consists both simply and importantly in a commitment to rigorous, unhampered, informed, critical study. Of necessity, this involves an equal commitment to what continues to be held as 'the disciplines' essential to a liberal education. Within this received notion, we see a justly inherited obligation to 'speak truth to power' especially in the sense of allowing critical inquiry to follow its course(s) wherever it (they) lead. In this received view of the liberal arts tradition, we see equally embedded the effort to develop throughout such institutions and all their participants the notion of a social conscience and a sense of purpose beyond the production of a 'disciplined' workforce and marketable technology. This course is undergirded, importantly and perhaps irreducibly, by the notion that a core purpose of such an education is the broadening of minds, not their limitation through specialization. And, given the many received notions of how HE is required to 'adapt' to the current many and varied contexts of globalization, one can ask whether the emphasis on this role in and for HE may in effect constitute a new and urgent role for the liberal arts.

In this regard, let us briefly quote Robert DiNapoli (2017) in his comment to an article by Tom Abeles on the necessary conjunction of HE and gaining access to work.

> Frankly, it is time that universities started to have more agency in leading the world instead of being led in a fast race towards self-destruction. This discourse about 'change' and the 'future' is tiring, often simply empty rhetoric used by managers to impose 'change'. And it robs academic life of its vital lymph: thinking time! Is the latter not a good to be pursued in everybody's interest, instead of racing at an ever-increasing pace towards ways of life whose dubious ethos is now imposed onto universities? Shouldn't we perhaps educate society to think more and more effectively?

It is both worthwhile and perhaps our obligation at this point in our history to ask ourselves a fundamental question, namely what 'space' have we been left with as HE practitioners to address the kinds of issues that surround our notions of 'the international' and the role of international students within the broader purview of HE? Do we, for example, see this latest 'nationalist turn' primarily as presenting a recruitment challenge to be met with greater marketing cunning to maintain our institutional income and not lose out to rising competition, as Marguerite Dennis (2017), for example, skillfully advises us to do? As an experienced university administrator, she is perhaps obliged to do so, but we wonder what space remains for us in our (traditional?) role as academics to raise and perhaps to challenge the underlying nationalist ideologies that are driving the current situation she addresses—perhaps, indeed, whether we are discouraged from doing so for fear of appearing too radical in questioning or challenging political and ideological positions, and thereby potentially jeopardizing our position in the market for international students. Earlier definitions of HE internationalization often included the comment that it could be regarded as a 'response' to globalization. We might ask whether this response has turned out to be more of a 'reaction,' determined by imperatives other than those that would constitute the critical and analytical 'response' of academia in its most distinctive role. On the other hand, we might argue that we should go beyond this and turn our critiques into something more active, taking a position and fighting a 'war' of our own choosing rather than one in which we may have been forced to participate against our professional instincts.

If the world is indeed facing the sort of existential crisis that we suggested in our comparison with the early twentieth century, but also crises associated with the rejection of scientific research such as that on climate change, then it is our duty in universities as providers of public goods rather than merely personal or commercial goods to take an action.

Finally, we wish to 'turn the discourse on its side' (as it were!). Where in fact are *international students* within this overall consideration and reconsideration of contemporary internationalism? The data tell us that for many years, despite the overall growth in their numbers (an average annual increase of 5.5% since 1999, reaching over 5 million by 2016—UIS 2019), they remain a very small portion of our overall worldwide student bodies, something in the nature of 2%. Perhaps our concern within HE should be to promote a far broader familiarity with and sophistication about internationalization by making it available to a majority of our students. It seems to us that in that context raising issues within HE about the intersect(s) between globalization and internationalization can become a primary discourse within the whole of the HE experience for all concerned.

NOTE

1. See, for example, Uuriintuya Batsaikhan and Zsolt Darvas (2017) for the point of view that has Europeans rediscovering the virtues of continued globalization.

REFERENCES

Altbach, Philip G., and Hans de Wit. 2015. Internationalization and Global Tension: Lessons from History. *Journal of Studies in International Education* 19 (1): 4–10.

Altbach, Philip G., and Hans de Wit. 2017. Trump and the Coming Revolution in Higher Education Internationalization. *International Higher Education* (89) (Spring). https://doi.org/10.6017/ihe.2017.89.9831.

Altbach, Philip G., and Hans de Wit. 2018. Are We Facing a Fundamental Challenge to Higher Education Internationalization? *International Higher Education* (93) (Spring). https://doi.org/10.6017/ihe.0.93.10414.

Ball, Stephen J. 2015. Living the Neo-Liberal University. *European Journal of Education* 50 (3): 258–261.

Batsaikhan, Rurintuya, and Zsolt Darvas. 2017. Europeans Rediscover Enthusiasm for Globalisation. Available at: http://bruegel.org/2017/05/europeans-rediscover-enthusiasm-for-globalisation/. Accessed December 5, 2018.

Collini, Stefan. 2012. *What Are Universities For?* London: Penguin.

Dennis, Marguerite. 2017. Luring Overseas Students in a More Nationalist World. *University World News.* Available at: https://www.universityworldnews.com/post.php?story=20170926141238242. Accessed March 12, 2019.

DiNapoli, Robert. 2017. *University World News* April 14, 2017 Issue No. 00455 http://www.universityworldnews.com/article.php?story=20170410195850403U.

Ferguson, Niall. 2009. *The War of the World.* London: Penguin.

Gills, Barry (ed.). 2001. *Globalization and the Politics of Resistance.* London: Routledge.

Knight, Jane. 2004. Internationalization Remodeled: Definition, Approaches, and Rationales. *Journal of Studies in International Education* 8 (1): 5–31.

Michaels, E., H. Handfield-Jones, and B. Axelrod. 2001. *The War for Talent.* Boston: Harvard Business Press.

Rowe, David M. 2005. The Tragedy of Liberalism: How Globalization Caused the First World War. *Security Studies* 14 (3): 407–447. Published Online February 23, 2011. Available at: https://www.tandfonline.com/doi/abs/10.1080/09636410500323153. Accessed February 12, 2018.

Stiglitz, Joseph E. 2016. *Globalization and Its Discontents Revisited: Anti-Globalization in the Era of Trump.* New York: W. W. Norton and Company Inc.

UIS (UNESCO Institute for Statistics). 2019. Available at: http://data.uis.unesco.org/. Accessed March 13, 2019.

Usher, Alex 2017. Nationalism and Higher Education. Available at: http://higheredstrategy.com/nationalism-higher-education/. Accessed October 30, 2018.

Williams, Joan C. 2017. *White Working Class: Over Coming Class Cluelessness in America.* Boston, MA: Harvard Business Review Press.

World Economic Forum. 2017. Theresa May at Davos 2017: Her Speech in Full. Available at: https://www.weforum.org/agenda/2017/01/theresa-may-at-davos-2017-her-speech-in-full. Accessed March 14, 2019.

CHAPTER 3

Understanding the Internationalization of Higher Education in South Korea with Different Theories of Development

Minho Yeom

INTRODUCTION

As a concept, 'the internationalization of higher education' (hereafter IHE) found its origin in the relationship between developed and developing countries. This concept can help to understand how the unequal higher education (HE) system of the world works in the development processes of countries, universities, and individuals. Developed countries and their universities are interested in spreading the intellectual and cultural assets they have accumulated, and developing countries and their universities try to accommodate the various types of intellectual and cultural assets built up by developed countries (Altbach and Knight 2007; Knight 2004). In this context, IHE can be linked to the concept of 'development,' which

M. Yeom (✉)
Department of Education, College of Education,
Chonnam National University, Gwangju, South Korea
e-mail: minho@chonnam.ac.kr

© The Author(s) 2019
D. E. Neubauer et al. (eds.), *Contesting Globalization
and Internationalization of Higher Education,*
International and Development Education,
https://doi.org/10.1007/978-3-030-26230-3_3

17

describes the process of transformation of organizations and individuals, wherein 'development' refers to the various activities that bring positive change or gradual growth to organizations and individuals (Collins English Dictionary 2018). The internationalization of *Korean higher education* can also be understood in the context of the political, economic, and social changes and development of Korea.

It may be inferred that Korea had already experienced IHE in various forms and contents at the individual, university, and government levels before the term IHE officially appeared in the academic world, because the structure and development of the Korean HE system have historically been greatly influenced by the political and economic effects of the surrounding great powers. Before the twentieth century, Korea had long been influenced by China and was subsequently impacted by Japan and the United States over the course of the twentieth century. During the Japanese colonial period (1910–1945), Japan sought to transplant the Japanese university system to Korea. During the US occupation (1945–1948), the United States transferred its HE system to Korea. Since the establishment of a nativist government (1948), Korea has organized and changed the Korean HE system again, based on the American model.

In short, IHE here refers to a variety of activities in which individuals, universities, and nations interact with and collaborate with foreign universities (Knight 2004). The core contents of exchange and cooperation among universities include research activities for the production of knowledge recognized as a primary purpose of universities and educational activities related to the propagation of produced knowledge. Research activities are focused on absorbing the knowledge and skills required for knowledge production, which can be a core resource for national economic development and social development, from advanced universities. Educational activities emphasize the acquisition of knowledge, skills, and attitudes necessary for the advancement of curriculum composition and teaching-learning methods to enhance the quality of HE. The acquisition of administrative knowledge and techniques related to university administration also constitutes part of the internationalization of content.

Altbach and Knight (2007) have argued that a primary purpose of IHE is directly related to the motivations of participants such as individuals/universities/governments, and their motivations overlap with each other. For example, individuals can participate in research and educational activities at foreign universities to expand their knowledge and skills in their areas of interest, as well as to secure learning opportunities for understanding the society, language, culture, and economy of the country in which they are involved. The purpose of individuals engaged in such processes is closely related to the maintenance and improvement of their social status (Kim 2011).

The purpose of IHE, as understood and practiced by specific universities and governments, has both a relatively macro- and ideological component as well as its practical dimension. IHE, as promoted by universities and governments, can be viewed as divided into two aspects: the realization of the essential value of the university and the engagement of economic interests. For example, from a historical point of view, universities in developing countries have sought to acquire the knowledge, skills, and culture necessary to advance them through exchange and cooperation with more advanced universities. This approach is an effort to respect and maximize the value and function of universities in the traditional sense. The economic view is a more recently focused consideration. IHE is a sort of systematic marketing that is carried out by certain advanced countries or advanced universities to attract foreign professors and students for the purpose of advancing their economic interests (Altbach and Knight 2007). IHE from an economic point of view is an approach adopted by developed countries and so-called corporate universities in the twenty-first-century modern society wherein such outcomes are seen as an intrinsic element of globalization.

Briefly looking at the internationalization phenomenon within Korean HE, its purpose as mentioned above is reflected in a complex and overlapping manner at individual, university, and government levels. For example, Korea is the country in which the largest number of students per 10,000 population engages with HEIs in the United States (Kim 2008, p. 69). On the personal level, IHE has been acknowledged as a means of maintaining and upgrading the social status of individuals and continues to have a strong influence within the population. The phenomenon of IHE-centering on US institutions, emphasized at the university level, has come to be the theoretical and practical basis for the development of the Korean HE system over the past 70 years. The IHE at the government level can be confirmed through two different positions taken by the Korean government during the process of national and university construction. At the core of this process, the government promoted IHE in the second half of the twentieth century after the establishment of the modern government in 1948 for a period of about 50 years from the point of view of the importing country that unilaterally accepted the presumed superior value of a Western HE system that could be gained through outbound-focused internationaliza-tion. In this overall process, the government focused on establishing its position as a supplier of HE expertise and value through inbound inter-nationalization, especially since the beginning of the twenty-first century (Byun and Kim 2011).

This chapter seeks to understand the current status and characteristics of Korean HE internationalization by drawing on different theories that explain the development process of countries, universities, and individuals. First, I briefly discuss four theories related to the concept of 'development': modernization theory, dependence theory, semi-periphery theory, and the social mobility effect theory of HE. Next, I present statistical data on four indicators that can explain the internationalization status of Korean HE and identify some characteristics based on the results of the theoretical review and statistical analysis. In conclusion, the characteristics of international-ization of Korean HE are discussed in terms of universality and specificity.

Reviewing Theories of Development Applicable for IHE

The phenomenon of IHE is directly related to the level of economic and social development of the country within which a particular university is situated, primarily because universities in the so-called developed countries have a presumptive comparative advantage in their research and teaching capacity compared to those in developing countries. In this context, apply-ing existing theories of development that explain the processes of economic and social change operating at both country and individual levels can help to better understand the nature of this phenomenon. Here, the concept of 'development' has two meanings, which seem to be slightly different but are closely interrelated (Cowen and Shenton 1996). First, development means advancing through intervention. Second, development is viewed as a form of transition to a capitalist system and results from the efforts of people to steadily improve their quality of life.

The main theories related to the concept of 'development' are modern-ization theory (neoliberalism), dependence theory, world-system theory (semi-periphery theory), and that focused on social mobility effects of HE. These four theories can serve as an analytical framework for understand-ing the perceptions and responses of the Korean government, universities, and Korean people in their various pursuits to IHE as it exists within the fundamentally unequal world HE system.

MODERNIZATION THEORY

The version of modernization theory, I employ, emerges out of the recent dynamics of state engagements focused on the constructs of neoliberalism (Thomas 2000). Notions of modernization have been at the core of mainstream social development theory that has been common to the collection of countries that have created and maintained the capitalist economic system since the 1950s. Modernization theory promotes the economic growth of poor countries based on their integration into a world capitalist system. Modernization seeks to liberate poor countries by improving on a range of sociocultural factors commonly associated with "traditional societies" that impede their development. Modernization theory is applied to HE policies pursuing economic growth mainly through government-led, top-down initiatives and policies.

The theory of modernization has been under constant change since its emergence in the 1950s and has increasingly become linked to the growth premises at the center of neoliberalism, which continues as the core of mainstream economic development today. Modernization theory has played a key role in how notions of economic development have been promoted, especially in the lesser developed countries, notions of how markets should be created and operate in such transitional societies, and ideas about appropriate means for the formation of the skills and attitudes necessary for knowledge production in such societies. Neoliberalism and the essential roles it assigns to marketization and privatization, so dominant in the late twentieth and early in the twenty-first centuries, are viewed as essential components in the promotion and achievement of economic growth, social development, and effective HE systems both in developed and developing countries (Trow 1970).

DEPENDENCE THEORY

Dependence theory has held a central and critical position within modernization and neoliberal theories (Paul 2016) of national development. Dependence theory focuses on the negative consequences that can and do arise from the acceptance and implementation of modernization theory. The theory of modernization has been particularly critiqued by the radical dependence theory that has emerged out of Marxist analysis since the 1970s. According to the dependency theorists, the social and economic underdevelopment identified in developing countries is the direct result of an active and unequal global process. From the perspective of dependence theory, poor countries continue to be underdeveloped, not because of a lack of necessary resources, but as a direct consequence of their historical colonial experience and the subsequent unequal roles they have been assigned in an international system of trade.

For example, advanced countries in the industrialized world are exporting their HE systems and knowledge production logic to developing countries, and universities in developing countries are therefore forced to rely on a knowledge production logic and HE system established by advanced universities (Altbach and Knight 2007). As a result, developing countries cannot form the logic of development or a HE system suitable for their own characteristics, and they are forced to be institutionally and mentally dependent on those of developed countries. These dependencies are manifested by the loss of subjectivity of developing countries in knowledge production and HE systems.

Semi-periphery Theory

Third, it is also possible to apply semi-peripheral theory to these analyses which was confirmed in the 2000s (Shi 2017). This approach is modeled on Asian countries that have achieved economic growth in the late twentieth and early twenty-first centuries, reflecting Wallerstein's world-system theory (Wallerstein 1974). He distinguished the world system as comprised of 'core / semi-periphery / periphery' to explain the economic disparities in the global labor market. The characteristics of semi-periphery theory question the claims of dependence theory and provide a theoretical framework to replace them.

Semi-periphery theory is recognized as an alternative to explain the changes in the world HE system resulting from rapid globalization since the late 1980s. According to these assertions, the border between developed and developing countries is blurred, and the middle zone between the center and the periphery is newly emerging. A concrete example is the HE system of the countries of the Asia-Pacific region that have achieved relatively recent economic growth including China, Hong Kong, Malaysia, Singapore, and South Korea. Developed countries classify these countries as major targets for investments in HE. Developed countries are strengthening their IHE in these countries through building overseas branch campuses or cooperative programs. These countries are moving from their past periphery status to semi-periphery positions, or they play a dual role as periphery and center in the periphery (Shi 2017).

SOCIAL MOBILITY EFFECTS OF HIGHER EDUCATION

Fourth, the internationalization phenomenon of HE is seen in connection with the desire for the social mobility of individuals (Kim 2011, 2015). If the three large theories mentioned above can be helpful in explaining the internationalization phenomenon on a macroscopic level, the internationalization of HE seen on an individual level is focused on the analysis of microscopic personal motivations. This approach sees that an individual's foreign degree obtained through internationalization has a global competitiveness dimension not only in the domestic job market but also in the overseas job market (Kim 2011). Thus, acquiring a degree in advanced countries directly contributes to expanding career opportunities as well as enhancing the social status of participants. In this context, individuals in developing countries recognize IHE as an opportunity to maximize human capital and the cultural capital of participants.

For example, knowledge, skills, creativity, and attitudes acquired from universities in advanced countries have a direct impact as human capital on individual labor productivity and lifetime income growth (Becker 1993). In addition, competent English communication skills acquired by individuals through internationalization serve as an important asset that can become pathways to joining international elites. This approach, which relates IHE to the social mobility of individuals, shows that the acquisition of degrees in advanced countries contributes directly to the accumulation of individual human capital, social capital and cultural capital. It also demonstrates that the processes and outcomes of HE internationalization work simultaneously at the local, national, and global levels (Kim 2015).

The four mentioned theories serve as useful frameworks for explaining the IHE phenomenon from a 'development' perspective both at the macro- and microscopic levels. In particular, the theory of modernization, dependence theory and semi-periphery theory that emerged in the mid- to late twentieth century can help explain the IHE phenomenon particularly in developing countries in a macroscopic way. On the other hand, the approach to IHE, which has a substantial impact on individual social mobility, has recently been recognized more appropriately as involving the relevance of HE effects. The motivation for each individual to approach

Table 3.1   Overseas Korean students in higher education institutions

Year	2007	2009	2011	2013	2015	2017
Students	217,959	240,949	262,465	227,126	214,696	239,824

Source KEDI (2017). http://kess.kedi.re.kr/index

Table 3.2   Overseas Korean students by countries

Year	USA	China	UK	Australia	Japan	Canada	New Zealand	Philippines	Others	Total
2017	61,007	73,240	11,065	16,770	15,457	8735	6060	13,257	34,233	239,824
(%)	25.4	30.5	4.6	7.0	6.4	3.6	2.5	5.5	14.3	100.0

Source KEDI (2017). http://kess.kedi.re.kr/index

IHE, whether in developed or developing countries, can help to understand and explain the IHE phenomena.

CURRENT STATUS OF IHE IN S. KOREA

Four indicators can be employed to explain the internationalization of Korean HE. The first is the number of students studying at overseas institutions of HE. The number of overseas students over a recent 11-year period increased from 217,959 in 2007 to 239,824 in 2017. The largest number of students in 2011 was 262,465, with an average of 232,221 students studying each year for the past 11 years (Table 3.1). Among them, students studying in the United States constitute an average of 25.4% of all overseas students (Table 3.2). This number is the highest in the world per 10 thousand people. This table also shows the percentage of students attending English-speaking countries. In 2017, the proportion of students studying in the United States, the United Kingdom, Australia, Canada, New Zealand, and the Philippines, as dominant English-speaking countries was close to 50%, at 48.6%.

Overseas students biased toward the United States have been a common feature that has been confirmed in Korean modern history, and it is also confirmed as a primary practice during the initial stage of nation-building. For example, from 1953 to 1961, the number of students studying overseas was 5406. Of this total, 4653 students studied in the United States, accounting for 86% of all international students (Jeong 1967, cited in Kim

Table 3.3 Foreign students in Korean higher education institutions

Year	2003	2005	2007	2009	2011	2013	2015	2017
Students	12,314	22,526	49,270	75,850	89,537	85,923	91,332	123,858

Source KEDI (2017). http://kess.kedi.re.kr/index

2018, p. 87). The results of the government-funded study abroad program for the past 40 years (1977–2017) also show similar phenomena (Ju 2018). The purpose of this system has been to support scholarships so that talented people selected by the government can learn advanced foreign cultures and contribute to national development. According to the National Institute for International Education in 2018 (cited in Ju 2018), among the 2440 students dispatched with government scholarships over the past 40 years, the United States (67.04%) has the highest percentage, followed by the United Kingdom (7.81%), Japan (2.87%), Russia (2.58%), China (2.45%), Germany (2.33%), and France (1.41%).

The second important datum is the number of international students attending domestic HEIs. The number of foreign students has increased about 10 times over the past 15 years since 2003, when the recording of data began. In 2003, the number was 12,314, rising to 123,858 in 2017 (Table 3.3). These data indicate clearly the characteristics of the internal-oriented internationalization that the government carried out in the 2000s. The government aims to expand the number of foreign students to 200,000 by the year 2020 and has implemented various policies to achieve this objective. Considering the current trend, the number of foreign students will continue to increase.

Third, it is the influence of the English language which is important in lectures and research conducted by major universities in Korea. Major universities in Korea have been obliged to provide English-medium lectures in undergraduate classes for more than 10 years and provide incentives for professors to publish English articles. In particular, the faculty's tendency to publish English papers explicitly underscores the power of English as a medium for both research and teaching. For example, the tendency of publishing articles in SCI journals by Seoul National University (SNU) professors, accepted as Korea's leading university, is an indicator of inter-nationalization trends in research at major universities in Korea (Table 3.4). The results of the last 10 years show that the numbers of articles published

Table 3.4   Research performance 2007–2016 at SNU

Year	2007	2008	2009	2010	2011	2012	2013	2014	2015	2016
SCI Journal	4324	4296	4475	5053	5395	5718	5996	6231	6994	6570
KCI Journal	2439	2177	2214	2401	2435	2318	2375	2428	2823	2430

Source SNU Statistics Annual Report (2010, 2013, 2015, 2017)

in SCI journals are about 2–2.7 times higher than the number of articles published in domestic journals. Major university faculty members, including those at SNU, place more importance on publishing articles in English journals than in domestic journals because the university and the government give more weight to publishing numbers of English papers and their citation (Cho 2016).

CHARACTERISTICS OF IHE IN S. KOREA

As we have seen from the previous statistical data, Korea is a country where many students have been studying abroad (especially the United States) since its liberation in 1945. Over the past decade, the government has been implementing policies to accommodate as many foreign students as possible. These two trends are evidence of a unique trend of IHE in Korea, although outward-oriented internationalization and internally oriented internationalization differ in size and content. Here, I discuss some of the significant features based on the analysis; these can be discussed in conjunction with the four theories related to a concept of 'development.'

A DUAL NATURE APPLICABLE TO BOTH MODERNIZATION AND DEPENDENCE THEORY

The results of the analysis of the internationalization status of Korean HE are relevant to both modernization and dependence theory and explain the process and results of 'development' in opposite directions. In particular, the internationalization of Korean HE's heavy bias toward the United States provides sufficient evidence to recognize the appropriateness of the theories, whichever position we take. This dual feature indicates that Korean HE internationalization is a substantial force in efforts to modernize the university system, even as it is overly dependent on the US HE system in other respects.

From the viewpoint of modernization, Korea has promoted industrialization based on the American model of capitalism during its modernization process and reconstructed and renovated the Korean HE system based on the American model. In the process, US-aid policies and US-centered study abroad programs were key drivers in establishing American academic foundations for Korea's HEIs. As shown in Table 3.2, the high percentage of Korean students in English-speaking countries is a clear indication of an internationalization tendency biased toward the United States. The Korean HE system accepted the American system as it was, and this was reflected in the composition of its undergraduate and graduate school systems. The undergraduate curriculum also accommodates the American system and experience in its quantitative composition and the distribution of academic majors and liberal arts subjects. The curriculum structure and operating system of graduate schools have also reached their present state in a form modeled after the American system.

From the standpoint of dependence theory, Korea has been heavily dependent on intellectual and cultural outcomes developed within the United States in the formation of the HE system and the development of its overall academic climate since its liberation from Japan. In the background has been a strong US influence in terms of Korea's direction and dynamics of both political and economic development processes, the elite status of students having American degrees, the importance of English in admission to education, and American hegemony in the global economy and geopolitics (Kim 2015). A typical example is the biased phenomenon of US degrees held by the professors of so-called prestigious universities. For example, as of 1999 in the case of the College of Social Science, 79 (77.4%) out of 102 professors in Seoul National University, 94 (89.5%) out of 105 professors in Yonsei University and 59 (67%) out of 88 professors in Korea University held US degrees (University Newspaper 1999, cited in Kim 2018, p. 250). Considering that professors specializing in social sciences are recognized as the key intellectuals in diagnosing the reality of Korean society and seeking alternatives, the fact that many of these major college faculty members were studying in the United States indicates the extent to which not only universities but also Korean society as a whole are very dependent on the United States.

The Relevance of Semi-peripheral Theory

In the twenty-first century, the type of IHE strongly promoted by the government indicates the possibility of applying the semi-periphery perspective and demonstrates the primacy of underpinning the system with an economic viewpoint, aspects of which are preeminent in recent trends of internationalization in practice. Especially in the 2000s, the changed position of the government within IHE reflects the transition from Korea as an existing importing country to that of being a supply country. The background of this change is Korea's increased international status, documented by its trade volume ranking within the world's top 10, economic growth over $ 30,000 GDP per capita, and the dramatic growth of popular culture including among others, K–pop. It also reflects the position of governments and universities emphasizing IHE for purposes of direct economic gain.

The government has determined that the outbound IHE has caused a serious national wealth outflow and is pursuing a policy of attracting foreign students to pursue the economic benefits that flow from their participation in the national economy. For example, statistics for the past decade (see Table 3.3) indicated that the number of foreign students studying at tertiary institutions in Korea reached 123,858 as of 2017 (KEDI 2017). In particular, universities are active in supplementing their lack of tuition income resulting from the decline in the domestic entering cohort by attracting foreign students, given that the contribution of international students to the expansion income of receiving universities is very substantial. From a theoretical point of view, recent government-led, inbound-oriented IHE models the characteristics of Asian countries whose growth is based on neoliberalism, entrepreneurship, and market-based performance. The Korean case shows that it is seeking to move away from its periphery status of the past and to transform itself into a core of the periphery. The Korean case shows the applicability of semi-periphery theory to IHE.

Key Means for Individuals' Social Mobility

The viewpoint of 'social mobility' linking the phenomenon of IHE with individual motivation can be recognized in the Korean case. The experiences of studying in the United States for Korean students is closely linked to individual social status competition (Kim 2011; 2015, p. 46). Korean students want to acquire a foreign degree (especially an American degree) in order to improve their social status and career opportunities. They pursue global cultural capital to stand out from competitors within domestic universities. Learning experiences at US universities provide Korean students with expertise, English competence and confidence, which result in strengths in getting better job opportunities at universities and businesses both at home and abroad. In particular, the comparative advantages of having an American degree in seeking a university professorship, or research and professional positions are confirmed through various channels. As indicated above, faculty positions at major universities in Korea are dominated by American degree holders. For Koreans, studying abroad is recognized as a key channel for individuals' achievement and social status.

Conclusion

This chapter demonstrates that the internationalization of Korean HE is the combined result of complex factors surrounding the effects of HE. These factors not only exist within the university but also its surrounding environments, including the political and economic growth processes of Korea, the development context of Korean universities, and the individual expectations developed within HE. For over 50 years since the middle of the twentieth century, the government has pursued IHE around the dominant context created by the United States in the course of its own national construction and university development. Universities have also actively accepted and imitated the university operating system and academic characteristics accumulated by American universities. Individuals recognize the strong influence of the United States that they directly and indirectly identify within the process of economic growth and social development, and in which they preemptively participate in IHE as a means of social mobility both on an individual level, and those that are confirmed in broader, more diffuse, effects experienced through other social engagements.

The Korean case indicates that the four theories that seek to explain the changes and development process of organizations and individuals and the applicability of each theory are supported in this dimension of social activity by statistical data and a few examples. In conclusion, I emphasize the phenomenon of IHE in Korea from the standpoint of both its universality and specificity dimensions. Here, universality means the characteristics of internationalization that are commonly identified within the global HE system. Specificity means contents that can be confirmed only through the case of Korea.

First, considering the universality of IHE, the Korean case reflects the level of political, economic and social influence between developed and developing countries. The universal characteristics identified in the Korean case show that national and social development and the improvement of individual social statuses are closely linked to IHE at the international, national and individual levels. From the viewpoint of modernization theory, the internationalization of Korean HE is recognized as a practical contribution to national economic growth and the establishment and development of the Korean HE system.

The Korean case also explains the effects of IHE on the individual dimensions of social mobility. The internationalization of Korean HE indicates that individual aspirations loom larger within individual career processes than elements of national influence. IHE in Korea is an important tool for maintaining and promoting the social status of individuals. In the meantime, the results of HE in Korea have played a key role in acquiring status and income for the middle class. In this process, studying abroad has played a key role as a ladder for individual social mobility. This is confirmed by the fact that university professors and graduate students utilize IHE as a concrete and practical means for improving their social status.

Second, in terms of specificity, the Korean case shows some exceptional characteristics. One is that the content and method of IHE is biased almost completely toward the United States model. This is confirmed at government, university, and individual levels. For example, Korea accepts the American model in its HE system, knowledge production structure, and curriculum composition and operation. The results reviewed above indicate the lack of diversity within the HE system. Another characteristic is that the internationalization of Korean HE shows the applicability of semi-periphery theory. A typical example is the number of domestic foreign students which has increased more than ten times over the last 15 years, reflecting both the economic growth and cultural improvements achieved by Korea.

The last characteristic is government-led IHE policies. Such policies have determined the direction and content of internationalization, and universities promote such internationalization in the form of passive responses to government-led policies. This characteristic indicates the degree to which the Korean political system has been maintained as a state-led authoritarian regime for the past 70 years. Specific evidence includes the outward-oriented internationalization that has been conducted by the government since the middle of the twentieth century and the inward-oriented internationalization that has proceeded in the twenty-first century.

This chapter has discussed the current status and characteristics of IHE in the Korean context by drawing on various theories explaining the development of countries, universities, and individuals. In particular, the theoretical review attempted in this chapter provides an opportunity to comprehensively identify the background, current status, and characteristics of IHE in Korea. This approach suggests that IHE is a result of a combination of individual, university, and governmental factors. These characteristics within the Korean case can be of particular help in re-conceptualizing future IHE dimensions and in building strategies for developing related programs.

References

Altbach, Phillip G., and Jane Knight. 2007. The Internationalization of Higher Education: Motivations and Realities. *Journal of Studies in Higher Education* 11 (3/4): 290–305.

Becker, Gary S. 1993. *Human Capital: A Theoretical and Empirical Analysis, with Special Reference to Education*, 3rd ed. Chicago: University of Chicago Press.

Byun, Ki-yong, and Min-jung Kim. 2011. Shifting Patterns of the Government's Polices for the Internationalization of Korean Higher Education. *Journal of Studies in International Education* 15 (5): 467–479.

Cho, Joo-hee. 2016. Responses to Globalization: Internationalization and Radical Shifts in University Environments. *Korean Journal of Educational Research* 54 (2): 341–372.

Collins English Dictionary. 2018. https://www.collinsdictionary.com/dictionary/english/development.

Cowen, Michale, and Robert W. Shenton. 1996. *Doctrines of Development*. London: Routledge.

Jeong, Bum-mo. 1967. The Influence of American Culture on Educational Exchange. *Research in Asia* 10 (2): 114.

Ju, Hyeon-ji. 2018. Studying Abroad for Tax: Holes in Government Sponsored Study Abroad System. *Daily UNN*. Available at: http://news.unn.net/news/articleView.html?idxno=191711. Accessed July 24, 2018.

Kim, Jong-young. 2008. In Pursuit of Global Cultural Capital: Analysis of Qualitative Interviews Revealing Korean Students' Motivations for Studying in the United States. *Korean Sociology* 42 (6): 68–105.

Kim, Jong-young. 2011. Aspiration for Global Cultural Capital in the Stratified Realm of Global Higher Education: Why Do Korean Students Go to US Graduate Schools. *British Journal of Sociology of Education* 32 (1): 109–126.

Kim, Jong-young. 2015. *The Ruled Rulers: The Study Abroad in the United States and the Birth of the Korean Elites*. Seoul: Dolbegae.

Kim, Jung-in. 2018. *University and Power: History of 100 Years of Korean Universities*. Seoul: Humanist.

Knight, Jane. 2004. Internationalization Remodeled: Definition, Approaches, and Rationales. *Journal of Studies in International Education* 8 (1): 5–31.

Korean Educational Development Institute (KEDI). 2017. Statistical Yearbook of Education (each year). Available at: http://kess.kedi.re.kr/index. Accessed June 20, 2018.

National Institute for International Education. 2018. *Study Abroad Scholarship Program*. Available at: http://www.niied.go.kr/contents.do?contentsNo=47& menuNo=289.

Paul, Abhijeet. 2016. Dependency Theory. In *The Encyclopedia of Empire*, ed. John Mackenzie, 1–2. Hoboken: Wiley. https://doi.org/10.1002/9781118455074.wbeoe242.

Shi, Xiaoguang. 2017. From a Periphery of the Centre to a Center in the Periphery: A New Direction of Internationalization of Higher Education in Asia Pacific Region. Paper presented at APHERP senior seminar, Lingnan University, Hong Kong, October 19–20.

SNU. 2010–2017. *SNU Statistics Annual Report*.

Thomas, Alan. 2000. Development as Practice in a Liberal Capitalist World. *Journal of International Development* 12: 773–787.

Trow, Martin. 1970. Reflections on the Transition from Mass to Universal Higher Education. *Daedalus* 99 (1): 1–42.

University Newspaper. 1999. *The Social Science of Korea Occupied by the United States*. Seoul: Seoul National University Press.

Wallerstein, Immanuel. 1974. The Rise and Future Demise of the World-Capitalist System: Concepts for Comparative Analysis. *Comparative Studies in Society and History* 16: 387–415.

CHAPTER 4

The Cultural Experiment at East Asian Universities

Rui Yang

INTRODUCTION

East Asian higher education (HE) has been fast improving in both quality and quantity. A modern HE system has been well established throughout the region. East Asia has become the world's third great zone of HE, science and innovation (Marginson 2014), and its universities are rigorously setting global quality research as their performance standard. With its unique traditions, East Asia is attempting to indigenize the Western university concept that has dominated the world for centuries. HE systems in East Asia have explored arduously an alternative model to combine Western and their own traditions (Yang 2016). Such developments look even more remarkable when compared with other non-Western societies. Looked at

R. Yang (✉)
Faculty of Education, University of Hong Kong, Hong Kong, China
e-mail: yangrui@hku.hk

© The Author(s) 2019
D. E. Neubauer et al. (eds.), *Contesting Globalization and Internationalization of Higher Education,*
International and Development Education,
https://doi.org/10.1007/978-3-030-26230-3_4

33

from a cultural perspective, East Asia's experiment in HE has significant theoretical and practical implications, both regionally and globally.

However, coming to terms with East Asia's HE development has turned out to be far more difficult than previously thought. The result of an assessment of the future development of East Asian higher education is far from certain. While various and even opposing views have been expressed, most studies have been overwhelmed by powerful economic and political influences. Few have adopted a perspective that gives sufficient weight to the impact of history and culture on contemporary development. Extreme views are usually held by external observers. Both optimistic and pessimistic assessments have cited East Asia's traditional culture as the reason for their arguments. For researchers within the region, although gains and losses appear to be more real, it has long been an arduous task for them to theorize how their universities differ from those in Western countries.

This chapter holds that HE development in East Asia faces fundamental cultural challenges, with a mix of traditional and Western values. What is reported on here is part of a project of a comparative policy analysis, focusing on the quest for world-class university status in the HE sectors of the Chinese mainland, Hong Kong, Taiwan, and Singapore. A case study approach was adopted, choosing in each society one comprehensive university and one technological university as cases. In each university, participants were drawn from both administrators and "grassroots" academics, first through professional contacts, and then by "snowball" sampling. The research used document analysis and in-depth semi-structured interviews to gather the reported data. Based on the major findings from that recent research project, this chapter points out emerging signs of hope and argues that East Asia is increasingly well positioned to get the mix right.

The Cultural Conditions of Higher Education Development in East Asia

During their ancient civilization for thousands of years, East Asian societies developed rich higher learning traditions that portrayed a unique Confucian way of thinking about human individuals, society, and nature as well as the relations among these entities. They first emerged in China. In sharp contrast to those in the West, their central focus was on political utility defined by the ruling class. East Asian ancient higher learning lacked an interest in seeking truth (as it came to be defined in a Western academic context) and focused mainly on knowledge of human society (Hayhoe 2001), characterized by close integration within a meritocratic bureaucracy that entrusted governance to those who could demonstrate their knowledge through written examinations. HE (as then understood) was to prepare officials for service to the state, and scholarly institutions were loyal servants of the emperor as a subsidiary body of the bureaucratic system. These traditions gradually became tremendously influential throughout East and some Southeast Asian societies especially in Korea, Japan, and Vietnam (Queen 1996). Although East Asian societies later had different HE development trajectories due to their different approaches to encountering the West, these traditions have remained powerful in shaping how people think and act in HE.

However, during the mid-nineteenth century East Asian intellectuals turned to the West for a new understanding of truth. The vast traditions were discontinued institutionally when modern HE systems were established throughout the region, patterned after Western experiences in terms of both their institutional infrastructure and underlying values. The Western-style system has no linkage to indigenous East Asian roots and thus allows little space for traditional values, although traditions remain omnipresent and ubiquitous in these societies. The incompatibility between traditional and Western value systems has led to a great divorce between institutions and practice at all levels in HE development within the region. As a result, East Asian societies have come to base their formal institutions on Western models and their informal system built on their own traditions. The fundamental differences between East Asian and Western ideas of a university have led to continuous conflicts, and East Asia's unique historical roots and cultural heritage have greatly constrained the functioning of core Western values that underlie the University. The continuous efforts and repeated failures to indigenize the Western concept of the University have been the bottleneck of East Asia's HE development (Altbach 1989). While manifestations differ from one society to another, none of them have successfully tackled such a fundamental issue.

For instance, together with a group of scholars from the Chinese mainland, Qian Mu (1895–1990) founded the New Asia College in Hong Kong in 1949 to preserve traditional Chinese culture and balance it with Western learning so that students might understand their cultural heritage while being able to cope with the challenges of the modern world. Such ideas later became the mission of the Chinese University of Hong Kong when the College became part of the University. During the past six decades, the New Asia College and the Chinese University of Hong Kong enjoyed both political freedom and financial affluence. Yet, the ideal to integrate Chinese and Western ideas has remained far remote. The conflict between the traditional Chinese emphasis on political pragmatism and the classical persistence in ontological significance of knowledge from the West has never been blended well. Instead, China's strong traditions in higher learning have long been a negative asset in the development of modern HE at both systemic and institutional levels. However, this is about to change.

While a modern knowledge system based almost entirely on Western experience has been well established throughout the region, East Asia is still greatly influenced by its traditional values that have been little reflected in the institutionalized system. Within the system, scholars and students find it very difficult to incorporate traditional values into daily teaching and learning. Even worse, they, as the product of such a system, have poor intellectual preparation to do so. Precisely for this reason, East Asia's modern universities have not been able to be as effective as their Western counterparts. Indeed, they are even soulless, lacking their own identity. On the one hand, Western cultural values underpin the operation of East Asian HEIs, as the intellectual environment in which East Asian university people are deeply embedded. However, these values are not sufficient for East Asians to feel settled. On the other hand, since the nineteenth century, the West has come to East Asia with such enormous prestige that few East Asians could articulate their traditions nowadays. The juxtaposition of the powerful influence of traditions and the overwhelming superiority of Western learning lead East Asian scholars and students to be trapped in a dilemma of choice. Despite the great economic achievement, East Asia still lacks a value system that could integrate both traditions sufficient to provide its people with a spiritual home.

The shift from traditional learning to Western knowledge is both ideological and institutional, as part of East Asia's wider profound social transformation since the modern times. The two dimensions could be viewed, respectively, as the mind and body of the shift. While the East Asian mind could and should never be entirely transformed according to Western experience, East Asia's contemporary institutionalized knowledge and values have been fundamentally Westernized. There has been a discrepancy between the already-transformed body and the under-transformed mind. The resulting legitimated knowledge often does not match socioeconomic realities, causing ideological confusion that has been in the making ever since the region's early encounters with the West in the nineteenth century. The confusion is especially evident among educated elites. While much has been trialed to indigenize the Western, little has been achieved. This has significant implications for East Asia's future development in culture and scholarship. Although itself a victim of such a mismatch, HE plays a special role here to bring together the aspects of traditional and Western philosophical heritages, especially in the current context of a revived intellectual consciousness (Jia 2015) and the much-changed features of contemporary knowledge.

New Realities of Contemporary Knowledge

As noted above, after a century-long absorbing of Western knowledge, East Asian societies have been institutionally Westernized, with an "academic colonization" of their intellectual mind (Hwang 2016). As a large-scale and yet fragmented process (Appadurai 1996), globalization has penetrated the deepest crevices of human endeavor. Many incongruous facets of human existence have been forced together into a giant tumbler, giving rise to contradictory, but also generative responses (Odora Hoppers 2009). In this sense, globalization is new, bringing all peoples into direct contact at all times for the first time in human history. "Previously excluded and excised 'objects' are now occupying intimate spaces with those who had believed that their subject position was ordained by God" (ibid., p. 609). Knowledge of and respect for others have become a basic condition for sustainability of any society. In such a dynamic episode, Western values are no longer seen as the only authority. Intellectual traditions of those excluded and epistemologically disenfranchised gain attention, acquire agency, and demand a new synthesis. There is an urgent need for an "integrative paradigm shift" (ibid., p. 602). As the moral and intellectual ground for coexistence and codetermination is fast increasing, questions around them are being asked at the most penetrating levels.

Featured by uncertainty, globalization is also an opportunity to develop new and different intellectual and academic discourses. It is increasingly likely to devise an intercultural understanding of knowledge from across cultures and civilizations to obviate a clash of civilizations (Gundara 2014). Despite great difficulties especially for non-Western societies, the possibility of re-imagining and re-designing education in the context of globalization is real. The processes of globalization of education need to be re-considered and re-analyzed. Change in the imaginaries and enactments of globalization can be initiated from every network node, as much in the United States as in East Asia—the networks are non-hierarchical and rhizomatic (Lundberg

2013). Human society has had Eurocentric (Bernal 1987), Indo-centric (Chaudhuri 1990), and Sino-centric (Hamashita 1988) memories, histories, and understandings of the past, which may not be a sufficient basis for future cross-cultural education and engagement. The attempt is not to replace one type of centrism with another, which reinforces centric intellectual tunnel visions, but to develop a more holistic and non-centric formulation of issues about the substance of intercultural and civic education (Gundara 2014).

Some propose to recognize "bonding" within a group and use this as a basis for bridging or linking with other groups on a sustained basis (Putnam et al. 2003). Gundara (2014), however, criticizes it as a prerogative of Eurocentric notions of the modern world system and essentially nineteenth-century constructions as articulated by Wallerstein (1974, 2006). He calls on educators to pool civilizational knowledge in ways that do not polarize peoples but help to develop more syncretism that recognizes difference and diversity, but also allows for the nurturing and development of points of mutuality and similarity between beliefs and values. Odora Hoppers (2009) stresses re-strengthening core values from different traditions of knowledge and living. In her eye, the assumption of superiority of the West and its patronizing obsession with facilitating the entry of traditional societies into the "developed" world is brought under sharp scrutiny. Western modernization progress and thought are only a temporary epoch in human history. She proposes re-engagement with the more holistic integrated conceptualizations of sustainable life held by cultures that have not been down the path of Westernization. It is a rapprochement of modern and older cultures, including modern culture's older roots where each complementing the other opens up the possibility of a viable future for humankind (Huntington 1996).

Both notions of "syncretism" and "rapprochement" are efforts to draw insights from other traditions and cultures from around the world and make them part of the global discourse. They aim to tackle transcultural relations that are complex, processual, and dynamic. According to Kraidy (2002), the local reception of global discourses and practices is necessarily a site of cultural mixture. Schools and universities are a space where intercultural and international communication practices are continuously negotiated in interactions of different power valences, vividly demonstrating how non-Western contexts encode Western representations. Hybridity is seen as a by-product of the transcultural dynamics between tradition and modernity as illustrated by Appadurai's (1996) notion of "disjuncture,"

Martín-Barbero's (1993) reformulation of the concept of "mediations," and García-Canclini's (1990) "cultural reconversion." As a site for conceptualizing global/local articulations, it emerges as a privileged characterization of cultural globalization (Fukuyama 1992; Huntington 1996). When the outside/inside distinction fails in a context of globalization, there is an intense search for ways to discuss, construct, and institute initiatives at local and global levels. It is a process of engaging with colonialism in a manner that produces a program for its dislocation (Prakash 1995), which is made possible not only by permitting subalterns direct space for engaging with the structures and manifestations of colonialism, but also by inserting into the discourse arena totally different meanings and registers from other traditions.

Where the above notions fall short is how they perceive the formation of the contemporary discourse of the *West* and the *non-West*, that is, how the West and the non-West are constituted and how *relations* between *Western* and non-*Western* societies come to be represented. While their intention has been well-taken, their approaches would not be effective. Indeed, they are intellectually inappropriate and practically misleading. Educational development in non-Western societies needs to be located into a coordinate system that includes the past, the present, the indigenous, and the foreign/Western, aiming at building their own knowledge systems that could provide their people with a spiritual homeland. Due to the fact that the West has come to the rest of the world with enormous prestige, the global knowledge landscape has been changed with Western knowledge at the center as the only putatively legitimate knowledge worldwide. The intellectual scenarios in non-Western societies have become highly complex. In contrast, the West has been the only one that has maintained its own conventional knowledge without essentially any fundamental external influences systemically. While it has been dominant on a global scale, it needs to learn from other civilizations to survive globalization. For non-Western societies, Western learning has become the most important part of their modern knowledge systems. Without Western knowledge, neither national nor individual development could be possible. Although the penetration of Western knowledge into every corner of non-Western societies has been profound, it is shocking to see how much people are still bogged down in a quagmire of a dichotomy between the West and the Rest. In this sense, a coordinate system that incorporates the past, the present, the traditional, and the Western is entailed.

The complexity is that the worldwide spread of Western influence has already become a precondition for nation-building in non-Western societies. It is no longer constructive to simply complain about this as "over-westernization." The realistic approach is to find new ways to incorporate the West without losing their cultural identities. Indeed, very few societies, if any, could afford to find ways without significantly incorporating Western knowledge and values. While unfair and unethical for many, such a situation has been caused by historical facts. It is thus more sensible to find ways to address it rather than simply trying to reject it. Non-Western societies are pressured to understand both Western and traditional knowledge thoroughly in order to conciliate both. Built upon Western experience, their education produces people with little knowledge of their own traditions which continue to influence the societies. Therefore, even when many educated people in non-Western societies are determined to achieve the integration, they are not well equipped to do so.

It is thus theoretically inappropriate and practically unconstructive to try to draw a dividing line between traditional and Western knowledge. Some scholars have long acknowledged this. For instance, Western theories and methods in social sciences have long become the basis for university curricula, including in the study of Chinese classics. By the 1930s, scholars studying Chinese literature all agreed that a thorough knowledge of both Chinese and Western literature was necessary to achieve innovation in literary research. As Fu Sinian (1896–1950) observed in 1919, "If you are to research Chinese literature, yet never understand foreign literature, or if you are to document the history of Chinese literature yet have never read any of the history of foreign literature, you will never ever grasp the truth" (Fu 2003, p. 1492). More recently, Bowden (2009) observes that while East and West have had their share of skirmishes and still have their differences, they have also influenced each other and borrowed heavily among themselves in the marketplace of ideas. This dimension of East–West relations is overlooked, even denied, when many speak of the history and ongoing relations between peoples of the East and those in the West. He highlights the common intellectual ground and the inevitable and unavoidable borrowing and exchange of ideas between the East, the West, and other traditions of thought.

For non-Western observers, the West is always present either explicitly or implicitly as the backdrop. Deep knowledge of both what they research and the corresponding situations in the West is always required. Shortage of one of them would lead to failures in both theory and practice in education. Unfortunately, their societies have rarely been able to have thorough knowledge of both. Even the most developed nations, such as Japan and Singapore, are still struggling with such a synthesis. For a country as powerful as China with rich historical heritage and remarkable economic development over recent decades, this has continued to be the greatest challenge. Liang Shuming (1893–1988) (Liang 1921/1990, p. 50) remarked in 1921 that "Chinese people will never gain a clear understanding if they only remain within the structures of Chinese society; if only they first look to others and then at themselves, then they will immediately understand." Today, China's leading scholars complain about the lack of understanding of the West on the one hand and even less knowledge of their own culture and society on the other by Chinese intellectuals (Zhao 2016). For those from a Western background, it is imperative to be aware that the modern rise of Europe was a result of borrowing ideas from other civilizations. Early interactions between Europe, the Middle East, and Asia were part of the development of the Renaissance and contributed to scientific and secular knowledge during the Enlightenment and led to Europe's modern rise. As Europeans in the last two centuries have unquestionably sat on top of the world, Western scholars are much less motivated to truly learn from others. With their limited knowledge of others, many of them are poorly situated to tackle issues in dealing with non-Western societies.

A Status-quo Analysis of East Asian Higher Education Development

For nearly two centuries, learning from the West has been a survival tool for East Asia's modernization of HE. To make Western-styled HE systems work in their societies has never been an easy experience. Unlike most Western HE systems that badly need to incorporate cultural values other than their own into institutional establishments, East Asia's priority is to integrate Western values with its own traditions. Based on the findings from my recent research project, I find that East Asia's century-long efforts are beginning to pay off. East Asian HE has shown increasing signs of obtaining the right cultural mix that has long been a particularly sticky business. Although little noticed, manifestations of current cultural transformations in East Asian HE are becoming increasingly visible.

First, the conventional gap between the ideas of a university in East Asia and the West is fast narrowing. Although the strikingly different value orientations, featured, respectively, by "working with (or even for) government"

(Yang 2018) and "speaking truth to power" in terms of a governance mode (Mora 2001), have led to constant conflicts in daily institutional operation and decision making in HE, East Asia's long-term diligent learning from the Western model has begun to bear fruit. Fundamental values underlying the University have begun to take their roots in the region. At the individual level, academics now widely cherish academic freedom dearly. East Asia's acceptance of such fundamental values has also been much institutionalized, with academic freedom and institutional autonomy popularly respected and even defended, especially by prestigious institutions. Even at the highest level of policy making in HE, the impact of such ideals is becoming more and more evident in most East Asian societies. Such progress calls into question mainstream views that predict an impasse of East Asia's HE development due to a complete lack of academic freedom and institutional autonomy.

In my fieldwork, the overwhelming majority of participants acknowledged growing autonomy granted by the government to their institutions. Understandably, some participants expressed their concerns about the corrupt role of traditional culture, especially the difficulties and obstacles it has caused in HE development. However, it is important to note that even those interviewees who emphasized traditional cultural values as a problem and called for "seeking truth and freedom" still agreed that much progress had been made. Such progress contributes to narrowing the conventional gap between Western and East Asian ideas of a university. They problematize much of the mainstream literature that has predicted an impasse of East Asia's HE development due to a complete lack of academic freedom and institutional autonomy. This contrasts with the changing government–university relationship in major Western societies where the state increasingly promises to "manage" creativity and innovation while the academic pursuit of truth gets itself entangled with the commercial pursuit of prosperity (Minogue 2001).

Second, East Asia is positioned to incorporate its cultural tradition in the development of HE. The participants tended to express their optimism openly and firmly. Even as some complained about their social, political, and institutional environments, they still placed much hope on future HE development in the region. This stands in line with the general scenario that East Asian people's attitudes to and knowledge of traditional culture have grown recently in a substantial way. Their own intellectual tradition has its strength and potential to contribute to the idea of a university. It offers favorable conditions for the combination of both East Asian and Western traditions. This provisional and open perspective allows East Asians to be able to appreciate opposing poles as a driving force and see opportunities in existing contradictions. The pragmatic approach to life further enables them to use whatever helpful means that are available to settle or solve problems or issues (Wong 2001). As for the idea of a university, they do not have to choose between the seemingly contradictory East Asian and Western university models. Instead, they can have ambivalence and flexibility to achieve an integration of both.

East Asia's HE elites and scholars believe the conflicts between traditional and Western values could be resolved, and although they could not provide an intellectual foundation for their confidence, their confidence is well based. The currently dominant model of the North American research university might be viewed as a house with rooms that are not connected to each other, caused by its close historical links to the industrialization process and which led to the segregation of specialist disciplines; of research and teaching; of knowledge transmission and the cultivation of character; and of university and society. East Asian culture could contribute to an increasing integration of humanity with the universe, balancing individuals, society, and the natural environment; of learning with life, balancing individual goals with national and global ones; of morality with knowledge, ensuring that moral formation is viewed as a core aspect of university education; of knowing and doing, which would foster capability for action as well as theoretical understanding; and of teaching and learning through a dialogic approach (Wang 2003).

Third, East Asian HE is clearly a mix of the East Asian and the Western in terms of knowledge and values. Modernization in the region as a latecomer involves a response to Western challenges. The desire to catch up with the West has always been fervent. Most recently, the striving for internationally competitive universities provides an impetus for East Asia's best institutions to follow the lead of European and North American universities and embrace "international" norms. All participants mentioned major global universities frequently and with no exception those were Western institutions. It was common to hear them refer to Western universities when talking about their international networks, strategic partners and positions in global rankings. The fact that all participants showed rich Western knowledge in their talks has to be understood in a context of contemporary East Asian society and culture that have been profoundly influenced by the West. Western learning has become part of East Asia's knowledge systems.

It is already impossible for East Asians to talk about education without mentioning the West.

With the new realities of knowledge production, distribution, and imbibition in an era of globalization, being able to learn from other cultures has become critically important for sustainable development of any society (Cheng 2007). Unlike the prestigious universities in the West where academics have poor knowledge of other parts of the world, East Asian academic elites know the West as well as their own societies. While Western universities operate in a monocultural (Western only) environment, East Asia's best universities work in a combined culture that at the very least includes East Asia and the West. Such a combination has become evident at the individual level and well established at the institutional level, while at the theoretical level it needs to be deepened much further. Signs of hope are already visible. This is not to say that East Asian universities will achieve their goals without twists and turns. Nor does it mean East Asia will necessarily succeed. Yet, the signs at minimum remind us that our conventional binary positioning of the East Asian and Western traditional ideas of a university need to be seriously interrogated.

Concluding Comments

For historical and cultural reasons, East Asia's experience of HE development compares sharply with those of Western societies. Since the nineteenth century, external values and knowledge have been imposed on East Asian peoples and societies. Therefore, East Asia's priority has long been to digest Western values and knowledge and integrate them with indigenous traditions. For most East Asians, this process has rarely been pleasant. Instead, it has been shot through with intense ideological and cultural conflicts. Yet, East Asia appears increasingly likely to be able to turn scars into stars. Signs are emerging to show how its longstanding efforts in learning from the West have begun to pay off. Both East Asian and Western traditions are incorporated deeply into the daily operation of elite East Asian universities. In this sense, East Asia is making a cultural experiment. Unlike their prestigious cousins in the West who have poor knowledge of other parts of the world, East Asian academic elites know the West as well as their own societies. Such a combination is globally significant and historically unprecedented.

Over the past decades, both achievements and difficulties in East Asia's HE development are substantial enough to challenge the existing literature.

No theory could fully capture the essence of what is actually happening in East Asian HE. Neither those within the region nor observers from outside could come to terms with East Asia's remarkable experiences and substantialize theoretically how and why East Asian experiences differ from those of Western universities. East Asia is to achieve further in integrating Western and traditional cultural values. Premier universities in East Asia are exploring an alternative path to future development with global implications. While it remains to be seen how East Asian HE will fare in the years to come, the experiment has already demonstrated the possibility of striking a balance between East Asian and Western ideas of a university that have been conventionally perceived as mutually exclusive. There is a need for new perspectives to observe the experiment, focusing on the cultural transformations of East Asia's elite universities.

References

Altbach, P. 1989. Twisted Roots: The Western Impact on Asian Higher Education. *Higher Education* 18 (1): 9–29.

Appadurai, A. 1996. *Modernity at Large Cultural Dimensions of Globalization.* Minneapolis, MN: University of Minnesota Press.

Bernal, M. 1987. *Black Athena.* London: Free Association Press.

Bowden, B. 2009. The Ebb and Flow of Peoples, Ideas and Innovations in the River of Inter-Civilizational Relations: Toward a Global History of Political Thought. In *Western Political Thought in Dialogue with Asia*, ed. T. Shogimen and C.J. Nederman, 87–107. Lanhan, MD: Lexington Books.

Chaudhuri, K. 1990. *Asia Before Europe: Economy and Civilization of the Indian Ocean from the Rise of Islam to 1750.* Cambridge: Cambridge University Press.

Cheng, C.Y. 2007. Philosophical Globalization as Reciprocal Valuation and Mutual Integration: Comments on the Papers of Tang Yijie and Roger Ames. In *Dialogue of Philosophies, Religions and Civilizations in the Era of Globalization*, ed. D.H. Zhao, 65–76. Washington, DC: The Council for Research in Values and Philosophy.

Fu, S.N. 2003. Review of Wang Guowei's Song-Yuan xiqu shi. In *Fu Sinian quanji* [Collections of Fu Sinian], ed. Z. S. Ouyang, 1492–1494. Changsha: Hunan Education Publishing House.

Fukuyama, F. 1992. *The End of History and the Last Man.* New York: Avon.

García-Canclini, N. 1990. Cultural Reconversion (H. Staver, Trans.). In *On Edge: The Crisis of Latin American Culture*, ed. G. Yúdice, J. Franco, and J. Flores, 29–44. Minneapolis: University of Minnesota Press.

Gundara, J. 2014. Global and Civilizational Knowledge: Eurocentrism, Intercultural Education and Civic Engagements. *Intercultural Education* 25 (2): 114–127.

Hamashita, T. 1988. The Tribute Trade System and Modern Asia. *The Toyo Bunko*, 46: 7–24. Tokyo: Memoirs of the Research Department of Toyo Bunko.

Hayhoe, R. 2001. Lesson from the Chinese Academy. In *Knowledge Across Cultures: A Contribution to Dialogue Among Civilisations*, ed. R. Hayhoe and J. Pan, 323–347. Hong Kong: Comparative Education Research Centre, The University of Hong Kong.

Huntington, S. 1996. *The Clash of Civilizations and the Remaking of World Order.* New York: Simon & Schuster.

Hwang, K.K. 2016. From Cultural Rehabilitation to Cultural Renaissance. In *Chinese Education Models in a Global Age*, ed. C.P. Chou and J. Spangler, 87–101. Singapore: Springer.

Jia, X. 2015. Research on History of Chinese Modern Academic Thought in Cultural Fever. *Lanzhou Academic Journal* 5 (1): 16–31.

Kraidy, M. 2002. Hybridity in Cultural Globalization. *Communication Theory* 12 (3): 316–339.

Liang, S. 1921/1990. Substance of Chinese Culture (*SUBS-CC*). In *Liang Shuming quanji* [Collections of Liang Shuming], ed. S.B. Zhang, 3–16. Jinan: Shandong People's Press.

Lundberg, A. 2013. Get Connected! Collaborative Adventures in Networked Spaces of Learning. *Proceedings of the Second International Conference of Emerging Paradigms in Business and Social Sciences*, 1–27.

Marginson, S. 2014. New Empires of Knowledge in East Asia. *Tsinghua Journal of Education* 35 (6): 1–12.

Martín-Barbero, J. 1993. *Communication, Culture and Hegemony: From the Media to Mediations.* London: Sage.

Minogue, K. 2001. The Collapse of the Academic in Britain. In *Buckingham at 25: Freeing the University from State Control*, ed. J. Tooley, 86–100. London: The Institute of Economic Affairs.

Mora, J.G. 2001. Governance and Management in the New University. *Tertiary Education and Management* 7 (2): 95–110.

Odora Hoppers, C. 2009. Education, Culture and Society in a Globalizing World: Implications for Comparative and International Education. *Compare: A Journal of Comparative and International Education* 39 (5): 601–614.

Prakash, G. 1995. Introduction: After Colonialism. In *After Colonialism: Imperial Histories and Post-colonial Displacements*, ed. G. Prakash, 3–20. Princeton, NJ: Princeton University Press.

Putnam, R., L. Feldstein, and D. Cohen. 2003. *Better Together: Restoring the American Community.* New York: Simon & Shuster.

Queen, S. 1996. *From Chronicle to Canon: The Hermeneutics of the Spring and Autumn Annals According to Tung Chung-shu*. Cambridge: Cambridge University Press.

Wallerstein, I. 1974. *The Modern World-System: Capitalist Agriculture and the Origins of the European World-Economy in the Sixteenth Century*. New York: Academic Press.

Wallerstein, I. 2006. *European Universalism: The Rhetoric of Power*. New York: The New Press.

Wang, Y.J. 2003. A New University Model for the New Century: From Perspectives of Chinese Philosophy. Paper Prepared for the Learning Conference 2003 Organized by the Institute of Education, University of London, July 15–18.

Wong, K.C. 2001. Chinese Culture and Leadership. *International Journal of Leadership in Education* 4 (4): 309–319.

Yang, R. 2016. Cultural Challenges Facing East Asian Higher Education: A Preliminary Assessment. In *The Palgrave Handbook of Asia Pacific Higher Education*, ed. C. Collins, J. Hawkins, M. Lee, and D. Neubauer, 227–245. New York: Palgrave Macmillan.

Yang, R. 2018. Emulating or Integrating? Modern Transformations of Chinese Higher Education. *Journal of Asian Public Policy*. https://doi.org/10.1080/17516234.2018.1448213.

Zhao, L.W. 2016. *China Sociology Yearbook 2011–2014*. Beijing: China Social Sciences Press.

CHAPTER 5

The Third Road Beyond Nationalism and Globalization? China's Belt and Road Initiative and Its Implications for Higher Education

Yue Kan and Bingna Xu

The increasing uncertainty brought on by the radical initiatives under Donald Trump's administration of the United States and the UK's disintegrating of the EU (Brexit) have brought about a hot debate on the role of nationalism in the current process of globalization. Meanwhile, a proliferation of anti-globalization sentiments has arisen especially after the unprecedented global financial crisis of 2008. Within this context, this chapter aims to elaborate how China's Belt and Road Imitative (BRI) can be seen as an example of how to mediate the conflicts between nationalism and globalization, and further, what implications BRI has for higher education (HE) in the future.

Y. Kan (✉) · B. Xu
Zhejiang University, Hangzhou, China
e-mail: kanyue@zju.edu.cn

© The Author(s) 2019   49
D. E. Neubauer et al. (eds.), *Contesting Globalization
and Internationalization of Higher Education*,
International and Development Education,
https://doi.org/10.1007/978-3-030-26230-3_5

GLOBALIZATION: A DOUBLE-EDGED SWORD

The past process of globalization is like a double-edged sword. On the one hand, it has promoted a dramatic increase of social and economic ties and interaction between various regions and countries. On the other hand, it has led to an unbalanced development between different parts of the world and inspired an anti-globalization trend that is only becoming more and more striking.

After World War II, the world entered the era of what many see as "Globalization 1.0," an age of continuing "mini-revolutions," which brought rapid economic, political and technological changes, such as open systems of trade, increased flows of information, and the spread of technology (Lee 2017; Barber 2016). At that time, globalization appeared to be a great success with rapid economic growth, millions escaping poverty (especially in developing countries), higher quality goods at lower prices, significant progress in industry sectors, steadily increased incomes, and expansion in trade, among other things. Nonetheless, it cannot be ignored that globalization has generated contradictory outcomes and indeed brought a great deal of problems, including great disparities in global incomes (Lee 2017), overlooking the flows of asylum seekers and economic refugees (van der Wende 2017), and imbalanced development among regions and countries (Jie 2017). As a consequence, it can be concluded that globalization leads at the same time to development and to underdevelopment, to inclusion and to exclusion, risking global economic imbalances with detrimental effects on social cohesion (Castells 2000).

After the 2008 global financial crash, the world economy entered a new phase in its evolution, "Globalization 2.0" (Barber 2016), and in Finbarr Livesey's (2017) interpretation, the era is causing a shift in priorities from globalization to localization, which is driven by technological change, consumer preferences, environmental challenges and nationalism. Gradually, as globalization recedes into angry and populist nationalism (Rodrik 2018), it faces great challenges, especially the anti-globalization sentiment that is actually a social movement critical of economic globalization. The UK's Brexit and the administration of Donald Trump in the United States are two well-known and typical examples of this. The UK and the United States, previously the loudest champions and major beneficiaries of a free-market global capitalism that has resulted in deepening and widening inequalities in growing segments of their populations who also feel fearful and disempowered, face an increasing racism and nativism that has gradually led to the rise of conservative jingoistic parties and moved the political pendulum rightward (Zeleza 2017).

Avigail Deutsch (2016) has pointed out that it was British nationalism that motivated Britain's vote to disassociate from the EU (Brexit) to protect its political liberties and invest efforts on its own, believing that the EU was infringing on their national rights in such areas as trade, economy, and immigration. Beginning as a straightforward and effective movement against EU, Brexit gradually extended to defend "Britishness" from the threat of foreign influence and metropolitan political correctness. Furthermore, the fears and frustrations concerned with globalization have been internalized into an embrace of national nativist identities (Bloom 2014).

Donald Trump, the 45th president of the United States, stressed "America First" and economic nationalism with a series of ridiculous actions including pushing for a US–Mexico border wall, enforcing a travel ban on selected countries, especially Muslim countries, canceling the Paris Climate Accord, ending the Trans-Pacific Partnership (TPP) trade deal, withdrawing from UNESCO and, more recently, threatening to impose tariffs of 45% on imported Chinese goods along with other tariffs imposed on countries that have been long viewed as "accepted" trading partners of the United States. These increasingly protectionist policies and decisions leave the impression that the United States is taking a step back from the world (Lehmacher 2016), and they may even have a potential "domino effect" as World Trade Organization (WTO) Director-General Roberto Azevedo has warned (Gao 2018).

These scenarios in the UK and United States were driven by a backlash against globalization and skepticism toward internationalization, both of which highlight the conflicting role nationalism plays in globalization. Within this context, nationalism has once again been in center stage and the increasing political fixation on national concerns comes with some deeply unpleasant baggage (Bloom 2014), raising the questions: what is the role of nationalism in globalization? Does stepping back from the world actually benefit countries?

Nationalism Vs. Globalization

Globalization has strongly influenced HE and has brought both positive and negative impacts during past decades. For instance, globalization facilitates cross-border mobility of both students and faculty and strengthens cooperation within regions and around the world. However, it also promotes the paradigm of a global knowledge economy, which has overly enhanced the global rankings competition for reputation, talent, and resources (Zeleza 2017; van der Wende 2017) and contributed to an imbalance of knowledge production, and global flows (Oyewole 2009; Zeleza 2017; UNESCO 2015). Nowadays, as anti-globalization sentiment continues, it is urgent for scholars and policymakers to reconsider how HE should respond to the backlash against globalization, and how to deal with nationalism and globalization as well as rethink the missions and values of HE altogether.

Avigail Deutsch (2016) argues that to tackle the problems caused by globalization, the West tends to take two distinctly opposite approaches: pursuing globalist policies while neglecting nationalism, or employing strict nationalism that shuns trade and economic relations with other countries. Obviously, the United States and the UK are adopting the latter in light of Trump's persistent initiatives and UK's Brexit.

In the UK (associated with Brexit), the United States, and the Netherlands, parties and factions at the extremes of the political spectrum are putting forward critical questions on the putative costs and benefits of international students, worrying about reduced opportunities and access for domestic students and calling for "domestic students first" (van der Wende 2017). This is consistent with opinions on academic nationalism and protectionism that emphasize that the mission of local and national HE should be oriented toward local and national needs rather than striving after global reputations, and that students ought to be trained for domestic labor markets based on local and national needs. Regarded as an English nationalist movement fueled by a mythology of England proudly "standing alone" (O'Toole 2016), Brexit was, in a way, predicted by George Orwell many years ago and was described as a danger with his very important caveat that nationalism is power hunger tempered by self-deception (Mathur 2017). What is more, George Orwell's conclusion should not be forgotten, namely that "the most necessary step is ... to raise the general level of public understanding: above all, to drive home the fact, which has never been properly grasped, that British prosperity depends largely on factors outside Britain" (Deacon 2016).

Actually, the vast majority of higher education institutions (HEIs) and scholars worry that as globalization tends to appear in retreat, several negative results may occur including a decline in market share of international students in the United States and UK (Mayhew 2017), a drop in academic rankings and HE prestige of HEIs in the United States and UK with rising global perceptions of the United States and UK toward intolerance and xenophobia (Altbach and de Wit 2017), less mobility of both students and faculty (EUA 2017), dissolution of the close ties of educational exchange and joint research projects (Mayhew 2017; Zeleza 2017), and funding shortages for HEIs (Highman 2017), among other things.

In response to Brexit, the European University Association (EUA) declared that "Britain universities will always be part of the European family and EUA will work together to ensure that the longstanding research and exchange relationships between Europe's universities continue" (Jørgensen 2017). In addition, other organizations have also shown their disapproving positions on Brexit. Christopher Ziguras, the president of the International Education Association (IEA) of Australia, described it as the final nail of "cool Britannia," demonstrating that a youthful, creative, and dynamic culture image open to the world no longer exists in the UK and wrote that,

> What seems to have died is the European international education community's faith in the inevitability of the cosmopolitan project, in which national boundaries and ethnic loyalties would dissolve over time to allow greater openness, diversity and a sense of global citizenship. (van der Wende 2017, p. 2).

His understanding of the importance of HE globalization is consistent with that of the European Association for International Education (EAIE), the International Association of Universities (IAU), and many other HEIs and scholars. EAIE and IAU propose similar visions and require HEIs to act as responsible global citizens and commit to help shape a global system of HE that values academic integrity, quality, equitable access and reciprocity, which demonstrates that they believe international education and exchange deepen appreciation of human society and are essential to the prosperity of societies and individuals alike (Ziguras 2016; IAU 2012). Thus, HEIs should align their strategies with their academic mission and values, engaging innovations and diverse students and addressing global problems in the manner that the new University of the Bahamas has proposed (Davis 2014). Their opinions implicitly indicate that they approve of the globalization of HE for it brings diversified values and inclusion toward an open society. As van der Wende (2007) stressed, HE shall broaden its mission for globalization to be more open and inclusive and shall balance economic and social responsiveness.

At the same time, some scholars hold a neutral attitude toward nationalism and globalization. In an article titled *Good and Bad Nationalism*, Robert B. Reich (2001) suggested that the nationalism aspect of a desire for political progress has both positive and negative effects on globalization. Nationalism in its positive effects can help build connections among countries and regions and contribute positively to the creation of a global village. Nationalism in its negative manifestations, however, can pose barriers toward global connections and unity. As a consequence, Reich argued that in facing globalization every country has to make a choice and it all depends on where the emphasis on nationalism is placed (Reich 2001). Moreover, Allan Goodman, the president and CEO of the Institute of International Education (IIE) has stated that actually nationalism and globalization are interdependent. He has argued that good nationalism drives HE sectors to build partnerships, attract international students in the interest of investing national human capital and economy and enhance globalization which in turn promotes nationalism (Goodman 2016).

Obviously, the two extreme reactions to globalization mentioned by Avigail Deutsch, namely extreme globalist policies or strict nationalism, do not work, and countries should, instead, find a way to balance globalization and nationalism, recognizing that for many, globalization is more fundamentally viewed as an irreversible trend. China's BRI, put forward by President Jinping Xi, has, according to many, been a great success that critically interlinks globalization and nationalism (Vangeli 2017; Jie 2017), demonstrating that nationalism can indeed coexist with globalization while also boosting the economy.

BRI and Upgraded Globalization

China's BRI, first promulgated by President Xi in 2013, comprises the Silk Road Economic Belt (SREB) and the twenty-first-century Maritime Silk Road (MSR) through a vast network of railways, roads, ports, and telecommunications infrastructure that aims to promote economic integration from East Asia, Southeast Asia, South Asia, West Asia, Central Asia, and Central and Eastern Europe. Featured by intra-regional elements and a wide-ranging coverage, BRI is framed by President Xi in terms of the values of peace and cooperation, openness and inclusiveness, mutual learning, and mutual benefit (Habib and Faulknor 2017). To promote connectivity, BRI mainly focuses on five major areas: policy coordination, facilitating connectivity, free trade, financial cooperation and people-to-people ties (NDRC et al. 2015). Among these efforts, infrastructure construction, including railways and highways, is the dominant feature of the New Silk Road with $125 billion in infrastructure projects, funded by a variety of institutions including the Asian Infrastructure Investment Bank (AIIB) and the Silk Road Fund (SRF) (International Lawyers Kingdom of Thailand 2018).

BRI calls for inclusive globalization, as *Vision and Actions on Jointly Building Silk Road Economic Belt and 21st-Century Maritime Silk Road*:

> BRI is designed to uphold the global free trade regime in the spirit of open regional cooperation by promoting free flow of economic factors, highly efficient allocation of resources and deep integration of markets, jointly creating open, inclusive and balanced regional economic cooperation networks, and seeking new models of international cooperation and global economic governance. (NDRC et al. 2015)

A great number of scholars think highly of China's BRI and consider it as "Globalization 2.0" (Barber 2016; Jie 2017), a Chinese model of globalization (Habib and Faulknor 2017; Mackerras 2017; van der Wende 2017) and new global governance (Albert 2017; Jie 2017), which helps the world enter its next phase of globalization (Gao 2018).

In terms of the debate over globalization and nationalism, BRI can organically interlink the global and the local. Aiming for win-win situations, BRI combines central state initiatives with regional and national development needs, so as to enhance the cross-regional coherence of BRI with locally adapted goals and guarantees a mutually beneficial set of outcomes. Moreover, BRI can align with the implementation of the UN's Sustainable Development Goals (SDGs) to confer substantial development profits and provide more global public goods (Horvath 2016). An example can be found in the way China and Thailand are pursuing cooperation in relation to the BRI. During "Thailand Big Strategic Move" Conference in June 2017, Dr. Somkid Jatusripitak, Deputy Prime Minister of Thailand, highlighted key strategic plans toward "Thailand 4.0," aiming for promising growth for the next twenty years, including the Thailand Future Fund, Public–Private Partnership (PPP) fast track, and the ten target industry cluster for the Eastern Economic Corridor (EEC), among other things. Dr. Jatusripitak stressed that Thailand will align with China's BRI to enhance economic stability and competitive capabilities (Jatusripitak 2017; Pr News 2017). Indeed, Thailand is already carrying out policies that are complementary to BRI, in which the EEC can be connected with the China-Indochina Peninsula Economic Corridor (CICPEC) mentioned in BRI (MFA 2017). Moreover, with a strategic location at the heart of the Association of Southeast Asian Nations (ASEAN), Thailand can bridge Asia with its neighboring countries and enhance regional connectivity. Therefore, BRI participates in the construction of EEC not only in order to deepen the China-Thai economic cooperation, but also to connect East Asia, South Asia, and ASEAN which collectively contribute to a proximately one-third of the global GDP (Pr News 2017). China-Thai cooperation under the context of BRI demonstrates that BRI can not only meet the demands of national and regional economic development but also, in turn, promote globalization.

The Implications of BRI to HE

There is no doubt that BRI is a regional strategy that upgrades various dimensions of globalization and critically interlinks the global and the local. More than just building roads, railways and port facilities, BRI also aims to build a community of shared interests, destinies, and responsibilities, which features economic integration and cultural inclusiveness (NDRC et al. 2015). BRI offers an immense opportunity for greater openness, further exchanges and deep integration in education at global, regional, and national levels. Education has a fundamental and guiding role to play in BRI, as educational exchange and cooperation are considered a significant part of BRI through its potential to develop talent and quality human resources. Unsurprisingly, BRI has a strong and far-reaching impact on HE, especially HE cooperation in the regions and countries alongside the route, raising the following questions: What role does HE play under the context of the BRI? Are there any priorities for HEIs in facilitating the goals of the BRI? How can the BRI help interlink globalization and nationalism in HE?

In this regard, China's Ministry of Education (MOE) has already made some efforts and has somewhat responded to the issues raised by these questions. The MOE developed the *Education Action Plan for the Belt and Road Initiative* in 2016, which expresses China's strong will to expand people-to-people exchanges and deepen cooperation in the cultivation of talent with the regions and the countries involved. It has also indicated its priorities for HEIs within the context of BRI. The first priority is to carry out cooperation to improve educational interconnectivity, such as strengthening coordination on education policy, facilitating smooth channels for educational cooperation, breaking language barriers among BRI countries, fostering closer people-to-people ties, and promoting the articulation of criteria for mutual recognition of academic credentials (MOE 2016a). The second priority is to deepen cooperation on cultivation and training of talent through four implementation programs: the Program of Silk Road Two-Way Student Exchange Enhancement, the Program of Silk Road Co-Operation in Running Educational Institutions and Programs Enhancement, the Program of Silk Road Teacher Training Enhancement, and the Program of Silk Road Joint Education and Training Enhancement (MOE 2016a).

BRI, also regarded as a vehicle for soft power which calls for stronger national efforts to link China's popularity and likeability to its meteoric rise, can enhance China's soft power by promoting a positive image of China around the world, and better communicate China's message as President Xi intends (Albert 2017). New tools of soft power, such as the Confucius institutes and various educational exchange programs, have been established by the BRI, which are helping to increase interaction and mutual understanding, and strengthen people-to-people ties. With 134 institutes in 51 countries alongside the route (*China Daily* 2016), Confucius institutes have already been a platform for cultural exchanges, beyond merely learning the Chinese language. Vice-Minister of Education Ping Hao has advocated that "the institutes have taken root in indigenous culture and carry out teachings and activities in accordance with local conditions, hence becoming popular and consolidating public trust along the route...develop bilingual talents, research-oriented professionals and vocational training personnel" (*China Daily* 2016).

In terms of educational exchange, the data from IIE illustrates that after the United States and UK, China ranks the third most popular destination for students who study abroad (Albert 2017) and attracts over 480,000 foreign students from 204 countries or regions to study each year, 65% of which are from BRI countries (MOE 2017a), although the number of students who earned Chinese government scholarships has constantly escalated. With a year-on-year growth of more than 11% (MOE 2016b), 58,600 (11.97%) foreign students were awarded Chinese government scholarships in 2017 (MOE 2017a), yet self-supported students far surpass those with scholarships (Fig. 5.1). As a consequence, to attract more high-quality foreign students, the Chinese government has launched several scholarship programs especially oriented to students from BRI countries, including the Silk Road Two-Way Student Exchange

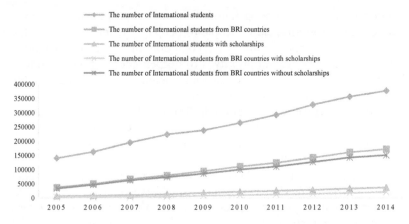

Fig. 5.1 The number of Chinese international students (2005–2014) (*Source* Department of International Cooperation and Exchanges, Ministry of Education, China. 2005–2014. *Report on Foreign Students in China*. Beijing: Ministry of Education of China)

Enhancement Program. The MOE has declared that BRI scholarships aim to maintain a balance between outbound and inbound students and facilitate cultural integration. It has proposed that over the next five years, 10,000 students from BRI countries will be sponsored to pursue degrees or short-term training in China (MOE 2016a).

Moreover, as of 2017, agreements on mutual recognition of academic degrees had been endorsed with 46 countries participating (MOE 2017b). Besides traditional forms of cooperation featuring exchange of students and international conferences, the MOE has proposed to widen and deepen educational exchanges and cooperation, including cooperation in mutual recognition of English proficiency levels, HEIs alliance construction, and an expansion of diversified cultural exchange with foreign counties.

CRITIQUES OF BRI

As of 2018, over 140 countries and organizations at international and regional levels have expressed their interest in the BRI and over 80 of them signed cooperation agreements with China (Gao 2018). Nevertheless, there still remains suspicion, resistance, and even public criticism in the international community toward BRI, even including some countries alongside the route. Is BRI a soft-power initiative? A hard-power initiative? Or a hard-power initiative wrapped in soft power? (Peterson Institute for International Economics 2016). Some even argue that BRI can be regarded as China's rise to hegemonic status (Bulloch 2017) or a geopolitical maneuver and point to the ineluctable problems BRI faces, including lack of a central coordination mechanism, potential conflicts among different beliefs, culture and social models, and the financial viability of cross-border projects (Huang 2016). Additionally, in terms of the role HE plays in strengthening people-to-people ties and soft power, this initiative suffers sharp criticism and rejection as China is pointed out to have disseminated its ideology through HE. For example, the Confucius Institutes, a powerful tool to spread Chinese culture and Chinese language, have been seen as "a Trojan horse for Chinese cultural infiltration" (Ying 2016), which are infused with propaganda and political influence with increasing concerns about the hiring policies, non-disclosure of contracts and lack of academic freedom in the curriculum (van der Wende and Zhu 2016). Moreover, Chinese HEIs have had difficulty attracting high-quality students, due to the limited number of national esteemed HEIs ranking among the world's top one hundred HEIs, the reputation of China's HEIs using pedagogic methods that emphasize rote memorization over independent thought development, and concerns over censorship by academics and HEI leadership of topics particularly relating to individual freedoms and democracy (Albert 2017). Moreover, there exist plenty of doubts and critics concerning BRI scholarships. Some scholars have predicted that BRI scholarships may turn out to be an utter failure because China pours large amounts of money to widen its geopolitical influence in the world rather than tackling urgent domestic issues and providing little benefits where needed (Pang 2016). Scholars in Hong Kong have even argued that the Chinese government, by dangling financial assistance, is trying to intrude into the independence of Hong Kong's education system (Yeung 2016).

CONCLUSION

Responding to the misunderstandings, suspicion, resistance, and criticism, Chinese President Jinping Xi has emphasized that "BRI is neither the post-World War II Marshall Plan nor a Chinese conspiracy" (Shepherd 2018) and stressed that BRI is rather more of a "spatial fix" than a geopolitical maneuver, and is not intended to challenge the realities of spheres of dominance in current geopolitical patterns, nor harbor any ambition to expand such spheres of dominance (Summers 2016). Undoubtedly, China is creating a Chinese model of globalization with the BRI within the global context of increasing uncertainty framed by the United States and UK's looming nationalism and backlash against globalization which offers global public goods to promote interconnectivity and bridge developing and developed economies, and also a shared vision for global development...all of which demonstrate China's commitment toward inclusive globalization. BRI, an innovative and ambitious regional development strategy, is a powerful platform for cooperation and communication. It offers opportunities to maximize development outcomes at global, regional, and national levels and to balance global and local needs. Although remaining misunderstandings, suspicion, resistance, and criticism exist, it pushes China to reconsider its priorities and also the challenges confronted so as to embrace a brighter prospect.

REFERENCES

Albert, Eleanor. 2017. *China's Big Bet on Soft Power.* Available at: https://www.cfr.org/backgrounder/chinas-big-bet-soft-power. Accessed March 30, 2018.

Altbach, Philip G., and Hans de Wit. 2017. Trump and the Coming Revolution in Higher Education Internationalization. *International Higher Education* 89: 3–5.

Barber, Lionel. 2016. *Globalisation 2.0—An Optimistic Outlook.* Available at: https://www.ft.com/content/3dffc316-bad3-11e5-b151-8e15c9a029fb. Accessed March 27, 2018.

Bloom, Peter. 2014. *As Anti-globalisation Policies Fail, Nationalism Sweeps the World.* Available at: https://theconversation.com/as-anti-globalisation-politics-fail-nationalism-sweeps-the-world-33102. Accessed April 6, 2018.

Bulloch, Douglas. 2017. *China's Belt and Road Initiative Does Not Support Globalization, So Much as Subvert It.* Available at: https://www.forbes.com/sites/douglasbulloch/2017/05/29/chinas-belt-and-road-initiative-does-not-support-globalisation-so-much-as-subvert-it/2/. Accessed April 1, 2018.

Castells, Manuel. 2000. *The Rise of the Network Society*, 2nd ed. Oxford, UK: Blackwell.

China Daily. 2016. *Confucius Institutes March on the Path of 'One Belt, One Road'.* Available at: http://usa.chinadaily.com.cn/world/2016-12/12/content_27643698.htm. Accessed April 13, 2018.

Davis, L.A. 2014. Nationalism, Internationalism and the Dawn of the New University of the Bahamas: Looking Ahead. *The International Journal of Bahamian Studies* 20 (2): 1–6.

Deacon, Michael. 2016. *How George Orwell Predicted Brexit.* Available at: https://www.telegraph.co.uk/opinion/2016/10/08/how-george-orwell-predicted-brexit/. Accessed April 15, 2018.

Deutsch, Avigail. 2016. *Nationalism: An Asset or Hindrance to Globalization?* Available at: http://www.globalethicsnetwork.org/profiles/blogsnationalism-an-asset-or-hindrance-to-globalization-1. Accessed April 1, 2018.

EUA (European University Association). 2017. *Brexit and European Higher Education Keynote.* Available at: http://www.europarl.europa.eu/cmsdata/123477/PowerPoint%20-%20JORGENSEN%20-%20Brexit%20and%20HE%20European%20Parliament.pdf. Accessed April 13, 2018.

Gao, Wencheng. 2018. *Boao Forum to Offer World an Asian Vision for Shared Prosperity.* Available at: http://www.xinhuanet.com/english/2018-04/08/c_137095328.htm. Accessed April 13, 2018.

Goodman, Allan. 2016. *Reflections on the Rise of Educational Nationalism.* Available at: http://items.ssrc.org/reflections-on-the-rise-of-educational-nationalism/. Accessed April 1, 2018.

Habib, Benjamin, and Viktor Faulknor. 2017. *The Belt and Road Initiative: China's Vision for Globalisation, Beijing-Style.* Available at: https://theconversation.com/the-belt-and-road-initiative-chinas-vision-for-globalisation-beijing-style-77705. Accessed April 3, 2018.

Highman, Ludovic. 2017. Brexit and the Issues Facing UK Higher Education. Centre for Global Higher Education Policy Briefings No. 2.

Horvath, Balazs. 2016. Identifying Development Dividends Along the Belt and Road Initiative: Complementarities and Synergies Between the Belt and Road Initiative and the Sustainable Development Goals. Scoping Paper for 2016 High-level Policy Forum on Global Governance "Belt and Road": A New Path to Regional Development.

Huang, Yiping. 2016. Understanding China's Belt & Road Initiative: Motivation, Framework and Assessment. *China Economic Review* 40: 314–321.

IAU (International Association of Universities). 2012. Affirming Academic Values in Internationalization of Higher Education: A Call for Action. Available at: https://iau-aiu.net/IMG/pdf/affirming_academic_values_in_internationalization_of_higher_education.pdf. Accessed March 30, 2018.

International Lawyers Kingdom of Thailand. 2018. *Seven Opportunities: Thailand and the One Belt, One Road Initiative.* International Lawyers Kingdom of Thailand. Available at: https://pugnatorius.com/obor/. Accessed April 5, 2018.

Jatusripitak, Somkid. 2017. *Keynote Speech: Thailand Big Strategic Move.* Available at: https://www.set.or.th/thbigmove/files/Session2_Dr_Somkid_en.pdf. Accessed April 9, 2018.

Jie, Jiang. 2017. *China's Belt and Road Initiative Ushers in 'Globalization 2.0':* *Experts.* Available at: http://en.people.cn/n3/2017/0412/c90000-9202011.html. Accessed April 3, 2018.

Jørgensen, Thomas Ekman. 2017. *Brexit and European Higher Education*. Available at: http://www.europarl.europa.eu/cmsdata/123477/PowerPoint%20-%20JORGENSEN%20-%20Brexit%20and%20HE%20European%20Parliament.pdf. Accessed April 13, 2018.

Lee, Gordon. 2017. *Nationalism: Globalization's Perfect Complement*. Available at: http://www.globalethicsnetwork.org/profiles/blogs/nationalism-globalization-s-perfect-complement. Accessed March 28, 2018.

Lehmacher, Wolfgang. 2016. *Why China Could Lead the Next Phase of Globalization?* Available at: https://www.weforum.org/agenda/2016/11/china-lead-globalization-after-united-states/. Accessed April 8, 2018.

Livesey, Finbarr. 2017. *From Global to Local: The Making of Things and the End of Globalisation*. London, UK: Pantheon.

Mackerras, Colin. 2017. *The Belt and Road to China-Based Globalization*. Available at: http://www.eastasiaforum.org/2017/08/31/the-belt-and-road-to-china-based-globalisation/. Accessed April 3, 2018.

Mathur, Vijay K. 2017. *Is Globalization Anti Nationalism?* Available at: https://www.huffingtonpost.com/entry/isglobalizationantinationalism_us_5970e3aae4b0f68541cd6320. Accessed April 9, 2018.

Mayhew, Ken. 2017. UK Higher Education and Brexit. *Oxford Review of Economic Policy* 33 (S1): 155–161.

MFA (Ministry of Foreign Affairs of Thailand). 2017. *Top Stories: Statement by the Minister of Foreign Affairs of the Kingdom of Thailand at the Belt and Road Forum for International Cooperation*. Available at: http://www.mfa.go.th/main/en/news3/6885/77698-Statement-by-the-Minister-of-Foreign-Affairs-of-th.html. Accessed April 3, 2018.

MOE (Ministry of Education of China). 2016a. *Education Action Plan for the Belt and Road Initiative*. Available at: https://eng.yidaiyilu.gov.cn/zchj/qwfb/30277.htm. Accessed March 25, 2018.

MOE (Ministry of Education of China). 2016b. *China Sees Rapid Rise in Foreign Students*. Available at: http://en.moe.gov.cn/News/Top_News/201611/t20161102_287359.html. Accessed April 11, 2018.

MOE (Ministry of Education of China). 2017a. Growing Number of Foreign Students Choosing to Study in China for a Degree Across Multiple Disciplines. Available at: http://en.moe.gov.cn/News/Top_News/201804/t20180403_332258.html. Accessed April 13, 2018.

MOE (Ministry of Education of China). 2017b. China Has Signed Agreements on Mutual Recognition of Academic Degrees with 46 Countries. Available at: http://www.moe.edu.cn/s78/A20/moe_863/201706/t20170620_307369.html. Accessed April 13, 2018.

NDRC (National Development and Reform Commission of China), MOFA (Ministry of Foreign Affairs of China) & MOC (Ministry of Commerce of China). 2015. *Vision and Actions on Jointly Building Silk Road Economic Belt and 21st*

Century Maritime Silk Road. Available at: https://eng.yidaiyilu.gov.cn/qwyw/qwfb/1084.htm. Accessed April 8, 2018.

O'Toole, Fintan. 2016. *Brexit Is Being Driven by English Nationalism and It Will End in Self-rule*. Available at: https://www.theguardian.com/commentisfree/2016/jun/18/england-eu-referendum-brexit. Accessed April 9, 2018.

Oyewole, Olusola. 2009. Internationalization and Its Implications for the Quality of Higher Education in Africa. *Higher Education Policy* 22: 319–329.

Pang, Ben. 2016. *Face Off: Should the 'One Belt, One Road' Scholarship Scheme Be Approved?* Available at: http://yp.scmp.com/over-to-you/article/103772/face-should-'one-belt-one-road'-scholarship-scheme-be-approved. Accessed March 27, 2018.

Peterson Institute for International Economics. 2016. *China's Belt and Road Initiative: Motives, Scope, and Challenges*. Available at: https://piie.com/system/files/documents/piieb16-2_1.pdf. Accessed July 1, 2018.

Pr News. 2017. *Thai PM to Showcase the Country's Strengths at "Thailand's Big Strategic Move"*. Available at: https://www.thailand-business-news.com/business/58221-thai-pm-showcase-countrys-strengths-thailands-big-strategic-move.html. Accessed April 12, 2018.

Reich, Robert B. 2001. *Good and Bad Nationalism*. Available at: http://prospect.org/article/good-and-bad-nationalism. Accessed April 12, 2018.

Rodrik, Dani. 2018. Populism and the Economics of Globalization. *Journal of International Business Policy*. https://doi.org/10.1057/s42214-018-0001-4.

Shepherd, Christian. 2018. *Belt and Road Initiative is not a Chinese Plot, Xi Says*. Available at: https://www.reuters.com/article/us-china-boao-bri/belt-and-road-initiative-is-not-a-chinese-plot-xi-says-idUSKBN1HI1HC. Accessed April 12, 2018.

Summers, Tim. 2016. China's 'New Silk Roads': Sub-National Regions and Networks of Global Political Economy. *Third World Quarterly* 37 (9): 1628–1643.

UNESCO. 2015. *UNESCO Science Report Towards 2030*. Paris, France: UNESCO.

van der Wende, Marijk. 2007. Internationalization of Higher Education in the OECD Countries: Challenges and Opportunities for the Coming Decade. *Journal of Studies in International Education* 11 (3–4): 274–289.

van der Wende, Marijk. 2017. Opening Up: Higher Education Systems in Global Perspective. *ESRC/HEFCE Center for Global Higher Education Working Paper Series* 22: 1–27.

van der Wende, Marijk, and Jiabin Zhu. 2016. *China: A Follower or Leader in Global Higher Education?* Berkeley: University of California, Center for Studies in Higher Education.

Vangeli, Anastas. 2017. *Is China the Potential Driver of a New Wave of Globalization?* Available at: http://theconversation.com/is-china-the-potential-driver-of-a-new-wave-of-globalisation-71575. Accessed April 1, 2018.

Yeung, S.C. 2016. *The Real Reason Behind Belt and Road Scholarship Program*. Available at: http://www.ejinsight.com/20160420-the-real-reason-behind-belt-and-road-scholarship-program/. Accessed April 7, 2018.

Ying, Wu. 2016. Review of the Confucius Institutes' Strategy for the Dissemination of Chinese Culture. *Chinese Education & Society* 49: 391–401.

Zeleza, P.T. 2017. Internationalization of Higher Education in the Era of Xenophobic Nationalisms. In *NAFSA 2017 Annual Conference and Expo*, May 31, Los Angeles, USA.

Ziguras, Christopher. 2016. *The Five Stages of Brexit Grief for Universities*. Available at: http://www.universityworldnews.com/article.php?story=20161012113345281. Accessed March 30, 2018.

CHAPTER 6

The Dialectics Between "Race to the Top" and "Back to Basics": Metaphors on Taiwan Higher Education Reforms Between 2006 and 2017

(Kent) Sheng Yao Cheng

INTRODUCTION

Global competition in the field of education has increased since the year 2000 with the appearance of international education surveys and ranking systems such as the Programme for International Student Assessment (PISA) and the Teaching and Learning International Survey (TALIS), both supported by OECD. The rise in competition internationally has led many countries to implement education reforms at the K-12 and higher education (HE) levels, reforms that represent a response to the new set of challenges the education sector faces in the era of globalization (Douglass 2016; National Center for Education Statistics 2017; OECD 2014).

(Kent) S. Y. Cheng (✉)
Graduate Institute of Education, National Chung Cheng University, Chiayi, Taiwan, Republic of China

© The Author(s) 2019   65
D. E. Neubauer et al. (eds.), *Contesting Globalization and Internationalization of Higher Education*, International and Development Education, https://doi.org/10.1007/978-3-030-26230-3_6

In the field of HE, pursuing global recognition and "world class university" status for institutions within their borders has become a priority for most countries in the Asia-Pacific region. To that end, many of these countries have released a series of education initiatives in the last two decades. For instance, the government in China formulated the Double First-Class Initiative in 2017 to support the development of 42 first-class universities and 465 first-class academic disciplines from 140 universities (Jacob et al. 2018). In Japan, the government implemented the Top Global University Project in 2014, involving 37 universities (Huang 2018; Nozaki 2017). Likewise, the South Korean government released the World-Class University Project from 2008 to 2012 to upgrade the global reputation of HE in South Korea (Jung et al. 2016; Hur and Bessey 2013).

In Taiwan, the Ministry of Education (MOE) first carried out the Five-Year and Fifty-Billion-NTD (New Taiwan Dollar) Project, subsequently named the Race to the World-Class University Project, in 2006, and followed with a second round in 2011 (Cheng 2016). However, there were many critiques of the program, including that it led to no change in college classroom instruction, no increase in internationalization, did not address public issues or the needs of local communities, and led to the homogenization of higher education institutions (HEIs). In response, the Taiwanese government released its newest HE initiative, the Higher Education Rooted Project, in 2017 that addressed these critiques (Cheng 2017). In this chapter, I provide an explanation of the Higher Education Rooted Project and highlight the importance of how to improve the public sphere of HE, encourage instructional innovation, develop special fields within universities, and engage the University Social Responsibilities (USR). To analyze HE changes in Taiwan during the last two decades, I borrow two concepts from US educational reforms, the Race to the Top (RTT) in 2009 and the Back to Basics initiative developed in the 1980s, as two metaphors to outline the dialectics between global competition and local demands. The chapter also highlights the debates between impact factors (IF) and social impact factors (SIF) of HE changes in Taiwan during the last two decades. Finally, the chapter concludes with some observations on the paradigm shift of HE reforms in Taiwan and their possible implications for other Asian-Pacific countries.

HIGHER EDUCATION REFORMS IN TAIWAN SINCE THE YEAR OF THE 2000S

Regarding the development of HE in Taiwan, Pochang Chen (2002) describes five distinct periods: the initial development period (1949–1953), the establishment period (1954–1971), the control and regulation period (1972–1985), the deregulation and open period (1986–1993), and the multiple autonomy period (1994–present). Moreover, the trend of HE in Taiwan in the last decade has been to focus on issues related to the access, equity, and capacity of HE, as the Taiwanese people have demanded in public demonstrations (such as the 410 Educational Reform Parade in 1994) and by public organizations (as in the Educational Reform Committee Report in 1996) (Yang and Cheng 2011). Since the year 2000, due to the increased global competition in HE that various international ranking systems inspired, the Taiwanese government started promoting its top 15–17 universities and research institutes through the Five-Year and Fifty-Billion-NTD Project (2006–2011) and the Race to the World-Class University Project (2011–2016) (Jacob et al. 2018). Most recently, in 2017, the Taiwanese government released its newest HE reform agenda named Higher Education Rooted Project that attempts to address concerns from the public about HE in Taiwan (Cheng 2017).

2006–2011: THE FIVE-YEAR AND FIFTY-BILLION-NTD PROJECT

Since 2000, pursuing excellence has been one of the foremost priorities of the Taiwanese government when it comes to HE (Cheng 2017). According to Dr. Mu-lin Lu (2006), the Political Deputy Minister of Education in Taiwan, the MOE directed special attention to policies regarding university assessment, instructional improvement, and other factors aimed at increasing university quality and prestige. Quality assurance is the key for enhancing the competitiveness of HE. Therefore, the MOE gave strong attention to the implementation and promotion of discipline and field assessments beginning in 2006. The MOE felt that by placing a systematic and cyclic assessment methodology into effect, that Taiwan's HEIs would be able to take their rightful place on the global stage (Cheng 2009).

The discipline/field assessments were conducted by the newly established Higher Education Evaluation and Accreditation Council of Taiwan (HEEACT) through self-evaluation reports and site visits. HEEACT would closely review each institution's quality control mechanisms to determine whether the set goals and objectives were reached. These assessments ran for five years, from January 2006 through December 2010. There were five major categories for the evaluation of HEIs: (1) mission, specialty, and self-improvement; (2) curriculum design and faculty teaching; (3) students' learning and students' affairs; (4) research and professional performance; and (5) performance of graduated students. The evaluations did not consider ranking or inter-institutional comparisons. They also attempted to combine the concepts of accreditation and quality assurance through peer reviews of the various departments and fields that were assessed (HEEACT 2007).

Generally speaking, the discipline/field assessments were intended to help institutions improve their instructional methods and enhance their academic strengths while also acting as a mechanism for self-evaluation, supporting each institution's continued commitment to quality, improvement, and excellence (HEEACT 2007).

2011–2016: RACE TO THE WORLD-CLASS UNIVERSITY PROJECT

Following the initial Five-Year and Fifty-Billion-NTD Project, the Taiwanese government adopted a second phase of the project from 2011 to 2016, which it named the Race to the World-Class University Project. Currently, in Taiwan, educational resources are insufficient to meet the challenges of rapid growth and competition in the HE sector, which, in turn, has affected the quality of education. The MOE addressed this issue by creating the Development of Outstanding University and Research Centers Project in 2011, which set a goal of establishing ten distinguished and outstanding research centers in Taiwan within five years and to have at least one university ranked as one of the top 100 universities globally, within ten years. The hope was to nurture and cultivate the academic talents of Taiwan as a means of increasing both the capacity and prestige of its higher education sector (Cheng 2009).

Years ago, many would think that these goals would be too difficult to reach. However, with the revision of the Higher Education Act, on December 13, 2005, Taiwan reached a significant education milestone; the MOE finally began assessments to ensure that the highest quality in HE research and teaching was being achieved. Through the implementation of these policies, the MOE is moving forward with its intentions to carefully prepare and place Taiwan's institutions of HE firmly on the international stage (Cheng 2009).

Debates on HE Reform Projects in Taiwan

After two phases of HE reform projects, there were plenty of critiques from the public on both the goals of the projects and the resource allocation that exemplified the previous decade. As a response, the government of Taiwan held seven forums on HE reform in 2016 and invited a host of HE scholars and administrators to discuss issues related to global competition and the pursuit of world-class university status (MOE 2017). During these forums, discussions focused on six crucial topics including: (1) How to effect instructional changes in universities, (2) how to respond to the demands of industrial innovation, (3) how to address the challenges posed by internationalization, (4) how to meet the needs of the public, (5) how to build connections with local communities, and (6) how to ensure that HE in Taiwan does not become homogenized, as many fear it will? (MOE 2017). According to the newest draft plan for the future of Taiwan's HE reform, the MOE intends to incorporate the advice received in the forums in order to increase the quality of HEIs such that they can attain world-class university and research institute status (MOE 2017).

The Higher Education Rooted Project, 2017

The most recent educational policy initiative released by the MOE in 2017, the Higher Education Rooted Project, draws on the topics discussed in the forums described above, by focusing on the five key struggles of HEIs in Taiwan: (1) improving instruction in HEIs, (2) meeting the demands of industrial innovation, (3) addressing the challenges posed by internationalization, (4) responding to the expectations of the public and of local communities, and (5) avoiding homogenization among HEIs in Taiwan. In an attempt to provide some possible solutions, the MOE has proposed five crucial policy orientations covering the public sphere of HE: the instruction innovation, the special fields of universities, the university's social responsibilities (USR), and a 20% grant for recruiting scholars and merit pay (MOE 2018) (Fig. 6.1).

Firstly, to encourage instructional innovation, the MOE hopes to enrich college students' fundamental competencies and career-ready abilities including multiple language communication, international and

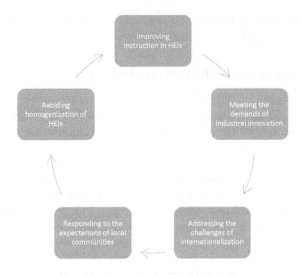

Fig. 6.1   Five struggles of HEIs in Taiwan (MOE 2018)

multicultural perspectives, information literacy, reasoning, innovation practice, and self-learning. Moreover, the government would like to strengthen the connections among industry, government, and schools and encourages the industrial sector to cultivate human capital and expand the availability of internship courses in order to help college students' employability (MOE 2018).

Secondly, the MOE in Taiwan has asked HEIs to further develop their own special fields and expertise. According to the new plan, universities are asked to determine their own mission and accountability indexes. Furthermore, it is suggested that they deepen their link to the industrial sector in innovative ways. At the same time, HEIs are encouraged to create more opportunities for international cooperation, for instance: constructing international learning environments, participating in international academic discussions, and increasing the amount of international exchange between faculty and students. In these ways, Taiwanese HEIs can potentially position themselves as top global universities and play a pioneering role in social innovation, value adding, and knowledge creation (MOE 2018).

Thirdly, improving the public sphere of HEIs is one of the major goals of the Higher Education Rooted Project. To address this issue, perspectives from students, faculty, and the system at large need to be taken into consideration. From the perspective of students, supporting disadvantaged students and increasing their upward social mobility through cooperation among government, industry, and schools are the most crucial issue. For faculty, decreasing the student–faculty ratio, recruiting high-quality faculty members, and taking care of special academic fields are the main foci of the upcoming Higher Education Rooted Project. Furthermore, on a system-wide level, important elements of the newest higher education reform agenda are to make institutional information more transparent, to strengthen institutional research, and to amply the HEIs' accountability (MOE 2018).

Finally, the MOE encourages HEIs to take on social responsibilities. HEIs have the opportunity to play a role in meeting the demands of local communities by practicing innovation and cooperation across various disciplines and institutions in order to assist in the development of the communities in which they are located (MOE 2018) (Table 6.1).

Metaphors from Back to Basics, No Child Left Behind, Race to the Top, Common Core, and Every Student Succeeds

To interpret the movement and transaction of HE changes in Taiwan, it would be helpful to adopt metaphors from the K-12 education reforms in the USA. To that end, crucial US educational changes including the set of policies known as *Back to Basics* in the 1970s, No Child Left Behind Act (NCLB) in 2001, RTT in 2009, Common Core State Standards (CCSS) in 2014, and Every Student Succeeds Act (ESSA) which are outlined below, based on the author's own research from 2015 (Cheng 2016).

Back to Basics

Ben Brodinsky (1977) has characterized the Back to Basics movement as including six elements:

1. In the elementary grades, an emphasis on the 3Rs, with phonics advocated for reading instruction,

Table 6.1 Accountability index for Higher Education Rooted (MOE 2018)

	Section	Index
Common index	Instructional innovation	• More than 50% of students take inter-disciplinary courses, minor courses, and problem posing courses • More than 50% of students take reasoning and programing courses • HEIs increase the innovation of the required courses' design and teaching to 15% • HEIs develop courses and labs to meet the needs of core industries • Numbers of faculty and students who participate the Innovation and Entrepreneurship Program increase 10% every year • More than 15% faculty are promoted through instructional research
	Public sphere of HEIs	• Increase the participation of disadvantaged students • Increase faculty salaries • Keep the HEIs' information open and transparent
	University social responsibilities	• HEIs participate in and build connections with development initiatives in communities where they are located and take on social responsibilities within those neighboring communities
Special index	Special fields of HEIs	• Cooperation between HEIs and the industrial sector • Increased international exchange • Expanded research capacity • Strength and benchmark
Competition index	Global competition	• 20% more every year for local students' international exchange participation • 10% more every year for international students' enrollment • 10% more every year for international scholars' teaching and research cooperation

2. In the secondary grades, devoting most of the day to English, science, math, and history,
3. At all levels, teachers take a dominant role, with "no nonsense" about pupils deciding the activities,
4. Enforcing strict discipline,
5. Implementing new promotion and graduation standards,
6. Eliminating curricular "frills" such as art, social services, and sex education.

Additionally, some schools introduced remedial programs in language arts and math or reintroduced phonics. Other schools took a more fundamental approach, stressing the 3Rs, requiring regular homework, and demanding neatness and decorum. At the time, these initiatives were favored by the public. In Philadelphia, for example, there were 17 such schools, which enjoyed wholehearted support from Black and Hispanic parents (Brodinsky 1977).

No Child Left Behind

The NCLB of 2001 is regarded as the most influential modification to date of the Elementary and Secondary Education Act (ESEA) of 1965 (ESEA 1965). The NCLB law, which grew out of concern that the American education system was no longer internationally competitive, significantly increased the federal role in holding schools responsible for the academic progress of all students. It put a special focus on ensuring that states and schools boost the performance of certain groups of students, such as English-language learners, students in special education, and poor and minority children, whose achievement, on average, trails their peers. If states and schools did not comply with the new requirements, they risked losing the federal funds they previously received through the Title I grant (NCLB 2002).

The NCLB law required states to test all students in reading and math in grades 3 through 8 and once again in high school. They were then required to report the results of those tests, for both the student population as a whole and for particular subgroups of students, including English-language learners, students in special education, racial minorities, and children from low-income families. Schools that received Title I funding (which was nearly all schools) were required to make Adequate Yearly

Progress (AYP) in test scores or face consequences such as state intervention or permanent school closures (NCLB 2002).

RACE TO THE TOP

The creation of the RTT federal grant in 2009 marked a historic moment in American education. This initiative offers bold incentives to states willing to spur systemic reform to improve teaching and learning in America's schools. The RTT ushered in significant change in the US education system, particularly in raising standards and aligning policies and structures to the goal of college and career readiness. It drove states nationwide to pursue higher standards, improve teacher effectiveness, use data effectively in the classroom, and adopt new strategies to help struggling schools (RTT 2009).

The four key criteria states were judged on for this competitive grant included: (1) the development and implementation of more rigorous standards and assessments; (2) the adoption of improved data systems to provide schools, teachers, and parents with information about student progress; (3) the creation and use of performance-based evaluations for teachers and school leaders to support job effectiveness; and (4) increased emphasis on and resources for innovative and rigorous interventions to turn around the lowest-performing schools. Inspired by this competition, many states adopted education policy reforms to increase their chances of winning money from the federal government; reforms targeted toward leveraging, enhancing, and improving classroom practices and resources (RTT 2009).

COMMON CORE STATE STANDARDS

The CCSS for English-language arts and mathematics articulated a baseline of content that all students across the country are expected to know by the time they complete each grade level. It was designed with the goal of preparing all students for success in college, career, and life by the time they graduate from high school (CCSS 2010). Creation of CCSS was also research—and evidence-based, and the priorities were that it be clear, understandable, and consistent, aligned with college and career expectations, based on rigorous content and application of knowledge through higher-order thinking skills, built upon the strengths and lessons of current state standards, and informed by other top performing countries in order to prepare all students for success in the global economy and society (CCSS 2010).

In addition to content standards, CCSS outlined processes through which students are to learn the material-processes that stress the kind of critical thinking, problem-solving, and analytical skills that will be required of them in college, career, and life (CCSS 2010). Ultimately, however, states were/are given the freedom to determine how to incorporate these elements into their existing standards for those subjects or whether to adopt them at all.

Every Student Succeeds

The newest educational reform in the USA, the Every Student Succeeds Act (ESSA), was passed in December 2015. It replaced its predecessor, the NCLB, and modified but did not eliminate provisions relating to the periodic standardized tests given to students—primarily by giving states greater flexibility in determining the type of tests they use and the other variables upon which school success would be evaluated. It also requires that schools offer college and career counseling and advanced placement courses to all students (ESSA 2015). Like NCLB, ESSA is a reauthorization of ESEA, passed both chambers of Congress with bipartisan support, and seeks to address disparities in student success based on race, income, disability, ethnicity, or proficiency in English that are evident in the USA.

Dialectics Between Race to the Top and Back to Basics

The way we think about and use HEIs has evolved from a system of liberal education, as defined by John Newman (1925), to the academic model of Humboldt University that highlights the academic and research orientation of the field of HE. Abraham Flexner subsequently proposed the idea of modern universities that combines the meanings of academic research and teaching (Barak and Kniker 2002). Subsequently, Clark Kerr (1993) argued that the contemporary university could be regarded as the City of Intellect. Many HE scholars have noted the phenomenon of HEIs transforming from elite to mass to universal and from research-oriented systems to social service-oriented systems (Carnoy 2000; Chen 2002; Douglass 2016; Frazer 1992; Green 1997; Hativa 2000). However, HEIs also represent an intellectual imperialism that involves the commercialization and prevalence of academic knowledge and a tendency to introduce managerial and business-oriented systems and personnel in pursuit of becoming world-class research universities (Hayes and Wynyard 2002; Henkel 2000).

A review of the K-12 educational reforms in the USA, including Back to Basic in the 1970s, NCLB in 2001, RTT in 2009, CCSS in 2014, and Every Student Succeeds Act in 2015, permits the use of the dialectics between RTT and Back to Basics as two metaphors to highlight the changes and development of HE in Taiwan since the year 2006.

Like RTT in the USA, the two phases of the Race to the World-Class University Project in Taiwan from 2006 to 2016 highlighted achieving excellence including the elements of academic reputation, employer reputation, faculty/student ratios, citations per faculty, international faculty ratios, and international student ratios.

Similarly, the Back to Basics movement can be likened to the triangulation of HE among research, teaching, and service. Moreover, Back to Basics was also an attempt to strike a balance between global/international competition and local/social demand. Furthermore, it promoted the search for excellence and innovation in instruction.

CONCLUSION

The changes to HE in Taiwan through the Race to the World-Class University Projects between 2006 and 2016, and, now, the Higher Education Rooted Project in 2017, can be understood as a similar process to that which the USA has been undertaking in their K-12 education reform. Through the dialectics between RTT, which highlighted global competition, and Back to Basics, which emphasized the idea/use of local demands, one can see that the search for a balance between attending to local communities and meeting global demands is a worldwide phenomenon.

This chapter promotes an effort to rethink the recent HE change in Taiwan, as represented by the Higher Education Rooted Project, by revisiting the role of HE among the golden triangulation of research, teaching, and service just as the 3Rs in the Back to Basics movement. The relationship between the three supposed functions of HE also emphasizes the conflicts between global forces and local demands. At the same time, the current Higher Education Rooted Project seeks to stress the importance of University Social Responsibilities (USR) and a dialogue over the academic impact factor (IF) to social impact factor (SIF).

REFERENCES

Barak, R.J., and C.R. Kniker. 2002. Benchmarking by State Higher Education Boards. In *Using Benchmarking to Inform Practice in Higher Education*, ed. B.E. Bender and J.H. Schuh, 93–102. San Francisco: Jossey-Bass.

Brodinsky, B. 1977. *Defining the Basics of American Education*. Bloomington, IN: Phi Delta Kappa Educational Foundation.

Carnoy, M. 2000. Globalization and Educational Reform. In *Globalization and Education*, ed. N. Stromquist and K. Monkman, 43–62. New York: Rowman & Littlefield.

Chen, P.C. 2002. *Higher Education Reform in Taiwan*. Los Angeles: Center for International and Development.

Cheng, S. 2009. Quality Assurance in Higher Education: The Taiwan Experience. In *Higher Education in Asia/Pacific*, ed. Terance W. Bigalke and Deane E. Neubauer, 133–148. New York: Palgrave Macmillan.

Cheng, S. 2016. A Study on the Educational Policies on Afterschool Programs and Educational Equity in Taiwan. In *Chinese Education Models in a Global Age*, ed. Chuing Chou and Jonathan Spangler, 65–75. Singapore: Springer.

Cheng, S. 2017. The Dialectics Between "Race to the Top" and "Back to the Basics": Paradigm Shifts on Taiwan Higher Education Reforms. Paper presented at the Asian Pacific Higher Education Senior Seminar, Lingnan University, Hong Kong.

Common Core State Standard (CCSS) (2010).

Douglass, J.A. 2016. *The New Flagship University: Changing the Paradigm from Global Ranking to National Relevancy*. New York: Palgrave Macmillan.

Elementary and Secondary Education Act (ESEA) (1965).

Every Student Succeed Act (ESSA) (2015).

Frazer, M. 1992. Quality Assurance in Higher Education. In *Quality Assurance in Higher Education*, ed. A. Craft, 9–25. London: The Falmer Press.

Green, A. 1997. *Education, Globalization, and the Nation State*. New York: St. Martin's Press.

Hativa, N. 2000. What Makes Good Teaching. In *Teaching for Effective Learning in Higher Education*, ed. N. Hativa, 9–24. London: Kluwer Academic.

Hayes, D., and R. Wynyard. 2002. Introduction. In *The McDonaldization of Higher Education*, ed. D. Haynes and R. Wynyard, 1–18. London: Bergin & Garvey.

HEEACT. 2007. *2006 Higher Education Evaluation Report*. Taipei: HEEACT.

Henkel, M. 2000. Identity in Academia. In *Academic Identities and Policy Change in Higher Education*, ed. M. Henkel, 13–25. London: Jessica Kingsley.

Huang, F.T. 2018. Higher Education Financing in Japan: Trends and Challenges. *International Journal of Educational Development* 58: 106–115.

Hur, J.Y., and D. Bessey. 2013. A Comparison of Higher Education Reform in South Korea and Germany. *Asia Pacific Education Review* 14 (2): 113–123.

Jacob, W.J., K.H. Mo, S.Y. Cheng, and W. Xiong. 2018. Changes in Chinese Higher Education: Financial Trends in China, Hong Kong, and Taiwan. *International Journal of Educational Development* 58: 64–85.

Jung, H., M.A. Pirog, and S.K. Lee. 2016. The Long-Run Labour Market Effects of Expanding Access to Higher Education in South Korea. *Journal of International Development* 28 (6): 974–990.

Kerr, C. 1993. *The Uses of the University*. London: Harvard University Press.

Lu, M. 2006. Opening Remarks. Paper presented at the Conference on University Classification, Ranking, and Quality Assurance, Tamkang University, Taiwan.

MOE. 2017. *Higher Education Rooted* (Draft Version). Taipei: Ministry of Education (MOE).

MOE. 2018. *Higher Education Rooted*. Taipei: Ministry of Education (MOE).

National Center for Education Statistics. 2017. *Financial Literacy of 15-Year-Olds: Results from PISA 2015*. Washington, DC: NCES.

Newman, J. 1925. *The Idea of a University*. London: Library of Alexandria.

No Child Left Behind Act of 2001 (NCLB) (2002).

Nozaki, Y. 2017. The Effects of Higher Education on Childrearing Fertility Behavior in Japan. *International Journal of Social Economics* 44 (5): 653–669.

OECD. 2014. *New Insights from TALIS 2013: Teaching and Learning in Primary and Upper Secondary Education*. Paris: OECD.

Race to the Top (RTT) (2009).

Yang, S.K., and S.Y. Cheng. 2011. Social Justice, Equal Access, and Stratification of Higher Education in Taiwan. In *Access, Equity, and Capacity in Asia-Pacific Higher Education*, ed. Deane E. Neubauer and Yoshiro Tanaka, 139–153. New York: Palgrave Macmillan.

CHAPTER 7

Globalization or Regionalization? Implications of the Reform of Japanese Higher Education in the Twenty-First Century

Shangbo Li

Introduction

In Japan, the trend of globalization in higher education (HE) began in the 1980s, accompanied by an increase of regionalization occasioned by more recent policy changes. Overall, HE in Japan in the twenty-first century has been characterized by change and exploration, the primary driving forces for which have been demographic: Japan's declining birth rate. According to the report, "*Future Estimated Population (the Whole Country of Japan)*," Japan's 18-year-old population had fallen to 1.2 million in 2017 and is predicted to further decline to about 1.03 million in 2030 and 880 thousand in 2040 (National Institute of Population and Social Security Research, October

S. Li (✉)
University of International Business and Economics, Beijing, China

© The Author(s) 2019
D. E. Neubauer et al. (eds.), *Contesting Globalization and Internationalization of Higher Education*,
International and Development Education,
https://doi.org/10.1007/978-3-030-26230-3_7

6, 2017). In the twenty-first century, Japanese society, long characterized as a "company-centered society," will face a huge challenge from such a reduced population. Another feature of this period is the transformation of the structure of HE. For example, as a part of its National Administration Reform,[1] Japan implemented a National University Corporation Reform on April 1, 2004, from which all the national universities, formerly part of the national administrative structure, were transformed into independent legal entities.

In this context in 2005, the Central Council for Education (CCE), the deliberative assembly of the Ministry of Education, Culture, Sports, Science and Technology (MEXT), commissioned a report entitled "On the Future of Higher Education in Japan" (2005 Report) and another requesting advice entitled "On the Future Conception of Higher Education in Japan" on March 6, 2017 (2017 Report). The 2005 Report suggested a framework for HE through 2020, and the 2017 Report examined the existing educational system and proposed changes for HE in the period through 2040. These two reports basically sketch the panorama and expected trends of HE in Japan in the first four decades of the twenty-first century.

Compared with the twentieth century, Japanese HE in the early portion of this period did exhibit some distinctive characteristics. Specifically, the Program for Top Global University Project in 2014, and the Program for Outstanding Graduate School in 2018 and Program for Designated National University in 2017 are representative examples of the move of the Japan government to accommodate elements of contemporary globalization. Within another focus, other MEXT policies have focused on "local national universities as places of vocational education" in 2016 and "restraints on expansion of universities in the twenty three wards of central Tokyo" in 2017 which can be seen as typical manifestations of national specificity. Furthermore, these reforms, while being led by the government, are based on the needs of industry, a characteristic feature of many governmental reforms.

Exploring this context, this chapter (1) focuses on the reforms that have taken place and (2) sets out to explore some of their implications, in order to clarify their impact in the context of overall patterns of HE development in East Asia. Sources used include Japanese government documents, data on Japanese HE, and the results of previous research.

The Framework of Higher Education Reform in the First Four Decades of the Twenty-First Century

The View Through 2020: 2005 Report

With the coming of the twenty-first century, the knowledge-based economy with its distinctive needs has gradually superseded that of the industrial economy, and society has more fully entered a genuine knowledge-based structure, which understandably places new emphasis on how people acquire and value such knowledge. In this context, the 2005 Report emphasized the framework for HE through 2020, regarding the university as its core. It underscored the importance of HE for the development and revitalization of the overall social economy and culture, and for a national strategy to ensure international competitiveness, while emphasizing that HE bears the critically important role of training prescient and creative talents.

Within this context, the report analyzed the trend line for the 18-year-old population and the changes in the quantity of HE available for their movement into HE, clarified the diverse functions, personality and characteristics of HE, mentioned the concrete measures to be taken to improve the quality of HE; the dynamics that seemingly now characterize various HE institutions in the twenty-first century; and the role of HE in society, etc. Remarkably, the report proposed to provide a differentiated financial support system according to the diversified functions emerging in twenty-first-century HE. As will be indicated below, this differentiated financial support system has been fully implemented within subsequent government initiatives in a manner that reinforces the differentiation of university functions promoted by MEXT.

The context of the 2005 Report lies in 18 previous reports on HE issued by the Council for Higher Education (CHE) (*Daigaku shingikai*)[2] in the 1990s, and perhaps most significantly, the October 1998 Council Report entitled "A Vision of Universities in the 21st Century," and a 2000 report entitled on "Higher Education in the Era of Globalization." In retrospect, the 2005 report has proved the more substantial of these various reports. It describes the overall framework Japanese HE should take leading up to 2020. Most importantly, the report also indicated an important emerging direction as it premised that MEXT's HE policy would transition from "making higher education policies and restraints" to "offering and leading the future blueprint." The statement clearly defines the functions of the university within this specified context. The projects described below are consistent with the notion of constructing higher-level research strongholds, acknowledging and promoting international exchanges, local contributions and so forth. Universities can choose to focus on one or more functions according to their actual situation and gradually help to realize an overall functional differentiation of all the universities in Japan.

REVISED BASIC ACT ON EDUCATION: ADDING THE "SOCIAL CONTRIBUTION" TO THE UNIVERSITY

In December 2006, the revised Basic Act on Education was implemented which is the first such revision of the law since 1947, adding new patriotic and university-relevant clauses. This framework mandated that universities be widely extended throughout society and that the resulting mission be recognized as the core of academic purpose. This was the first effort to define the "social contribution" function of the university in the Basic Act on Education over a 59 year period.

The Future Vision Before 2040: 2017 Report

This document clearly illustrated the reality that MEXT had become the definitive administrative body in the formulation and implementation of Japan education policies including HE. Since the end of the Second World War, MEXT has played an increasingly important guiding role in the overall development of education and research.

Recognizing this role, on September 12, 2014, the prime minister and his cabinet proposed that in order to solve the problem of a rapid population reduction and the phenomenon of super-aging, government should work together to make full use of the characteristics of all regions of the country and create a self-disciplined and sustainable society (https://www.kantei.go.jp/jp/headline/chihou_sousei/). The proposal made clear that accomplishing such major national changes was the central responsibility of MEXT and would clearly help define essential features of Japanese society.

In 2014, the Town, People, and Work Law was introduced within this framework, followed in December 2016 by a subsequent "Comprehensive Recreation Strategy on Town, People, and Work (2016 Review Vision)" (https://www.kantei.go.jp/jp/singi/sousei/info/) which was approved by the Cabinet.[3] The strategy contained within it linked a comprehensive discussion of the development of local universities with strict controls on new increases in university functions undertaken within Tokyo, and promoting the transfer of some Tokyo-centered activities to other local settings, intended to develop new perspectives within educational policy overall, and to locate new directions within such measures before the summer of 2017. In this manner, the government was requesting that these issues be considered in a subsequent 2017 Report.

Correspondingly, in March 2017, the minister commissioned MEXT to consider four issues from a mid-long-term perspective, with a view toward their realization within Japanese society before 2040. The four are: strengthening the functions of HEIs, improving overall HE quality, ensuring the opportunity to provide high-quality HE for local areas, and supporting an overall reform of HE. It can be said that the report released at the end of the year is the summary of extensive CCE deliberations. After analyzing various changes in the overall social structure, the report emphasizes that the cultivating of talents in HE should be based on the traditional college cohort combined with the increased participation of the working adult student in recognition of the shrinking 18-year-old population. With respect to educational research, the report emphasizes the interdependence of education, research, student activity, and management as central to a coherent overall education policy. It also emphasizes the problem of HE quality assurance and information disclosure and stresses that given the reality of the shrinking college cohort, national, public, and private universities should strengthen their cooperation with local governments and industries, in order to build a lasting system to revitalize local social and economic development. In other words, "working adult students" and "local" both are priorities for solving the problem of the decreasing 18-year-old population.

GLOBALIZATION OR REGIONALIZATION? RESEARCH STRONGHOLDS, INTERNATIONAL EXCHANGE, AND FUNCTIONAL DIFFERENTIATION OF THE UNIVERSITY

Research Strongholds

Foremost among the projects undertaken by MEXT over the past decade to build and improve the global competitiveness of Japan's universities have been the following:

The 21st Century Center of Excellence Program (2002–2008); the Program for Characteristic Good Practice (2003–2007); the Program for Attractive Graduate School Education Initiative (2005–2006); the Program for Graduate School Good Practice (2007–2013); the Program for Global Centers of Excellence (2007–2013); the Program for Promoting High-Quality University Education (2008–2011); the Project for Establishing University Network for Internationalization (Top 30) (2009–2014); the World Premier International Research Center Initiative (2007–); the Inter-University Exchange Program (2011–); the Program for Leading Graduate Schools (2011–); the "Top Global University Project" (2014–); the Third Medium-Term Plan for "Designated National University" (2017–); the Program for "Outstanding Graduate School" (2018–), etc. At present, the first seven have been completed with the remaining six projects in the implementation or initiation stages.

The objectives of these many projects supported by government funds can be roughly divided into three: building high-level research strongholds, enhancing international exchange, and promoting the functional differentiation of universities. Creating research strongholds, sustaining international competitiveness and the differentiation between universities are the three most basic underlying elements.

According to the Report on School Basic Survey issued by MEXT in 2014, at that time there were 600,000 undergraduates, 73,000 masters and 15,400 doctoral candidates in Japan. The government has implemented several projects for the top graduate schools within the educational pyramid to support a high-level research base. The 21st Century Center of Excellence Program (2002–2008) supported 274 programs in 91 universities; the Global COE Program (2007–2013) supported 140 programs in 41 universities; and the Program for Leading Graduate Schools (2011–) supports 62 programs in 30 universities. Meanwhile, the World Premier International Research Center Initiative (2007–) and the Program for Excellent Graduate School(s) (2018–) have been and will continue to provide government financial support for the establishment of high-level research strongholds aimed at meeting world quality levels. In addition, the Program for Designated National Universities (2017–) selected the University of Tokyo, Kyoto University and Tohoku University as the three institutions designated to carry out research at the level of the world's best research universities.

International Exchange

According to the Report on Basic School Survey of 2017, the number of Japanese students studying aboard reached a peak at 83,000 in 2004, and since that point has generated no obvious increase. In Japan, for a long time, the number of students studying abroad and the number of hosting international students have both been regarded as important indicators of university internationalization. The main purposes of these projects, such as the Project for Establishing University Network for Internationalization (Top 30) (2009–2014), the World Premier International Research Center Initiative (2007–), and the Inter-University Exchange Program (2011–), have been to obtain and cultivate excellent talents and enhance Japan's global competitiveness. The implementation of these projects also promotes the interaction and communication between Japanese and foreign students. For instance, the Inter-University Exchange Program (2011–) is aimed at contributing to hosting 300,000 international students and sending 120,000 Japanese students to study abroad by 2020.

Functional Differentiation of Universities

A particularly noteworthy change in many projects is the Third Medium-Term Plan for function differentiation of national universities. Since 2004, Japan has initiated the reform of national universities at the corporate level, taking six years as a cycle, and is currently entering the third cycle (2016–2021) with the medium-term plan promulgated in 2016. In this new medium-term plan, MEXT divided 86 national universities into three groups[4]: classifying 16 universities as "world excellence," 15 universities as having "excellent features," and 55 universities as making "regional contributions." The government's financial budget has also been distributed according to these three categories. In the future, 16 "world excellence" universities will be the main element of Japan's participation in global competition; 15 "excellent feature" universities will be viewed as distinctive high-level universities in Japan; and the 55 other universities belong to the "local contribution" category and will mainly focus on talent training for local industry revitalization. It could be argued that the 55 universities will become the core force of regionalization of national universities.

Another change affecting private universities took place in Tokyo in 2018. On February 23, 2018, MEXT issued a new standard for the establishment of a university, which stipulates that from 2019 onward, private universities in the 23 Districts of Tokyo will not be allowed to increase their enrollment levels and/or create new departments—an effort to prevent young people from concentrating too much in Tokyo, help the development of other local universities, revitalize local industries and develop local economies. According to the statistics of the Ministry of Internal Affairs and Communication (MIC) and MEXT (*Mainichi Shinbun* 2018), in October 2016, 28.6% of the total population of 126,933,000 people, 28.7% of 777 universities, and 40.8% of 2,873,624 university students were all concentrated in the Tokyo Area.[5] The government plans to control the excess concentration of university students and universities in the Tokyo metropolitan area and proposed legislation to this effect in January 2018. It follows from this official proposal that over the next ten years, the government will not allow Tokyo's universities to recruit more students, contributing to the goal of revitalizing local universities and helping local authorities support their backbone industries. The bill is expected to be enacted in the Diet session (current as of this writing). According to the 2017 Report, there are many small private universities in local areas, and the number of with dissatisfied students has reached 40% of the total, often students of small private universities. It is difficult for local universities to reach their desired numbers of recruited students. This was a major focus of MEXT's effort to develop standards that emerged as: "Restraint on Expansion of Universities in the Twenty Three Districts of Central Tokyo." As suggested above, MEXT will no longer allow private universities to increase their enrollment and add new departments in this area after the 2019 fiscal year. According to the "Comprehensive Recreation Strategy on Town, People, and Work (2017 Review Vision)," the Japanese population reached a peak in 126,933,000 in 2008, with the total population figure reduced by 162,000 in 2017 from that of 2016. This overall empirical population has continued to decline over the past six years.

THE REFORM OF JAPANESE HIGHER EDUCATION IN THE TWENTY-FIRST CENTURY

Changing in the Humboldt View of University

The above analysis outlines roughly the new movement of Japanese HE for the first 40 years of the twenty-first century. In particular, the implementation of the Revised Basic Act on Education in 2006 added a new "social contribution" category to the mission of universities, which has had a major impact on university faculties who have been positioned within an accepted notion of "collegiate purpose" for decades after the Second World War.

As the 2005 Report pointed out, the concept of Humboldt's Idea of the university developed in nineteenth-century Germany had a profound influence on Japanese HE during its transition from the elite to the mass stage (Ushiogi 2008). For a very extended period university, faculty members have regarded themselves as primarily researchers and accepted the premise that publishing their own research results constituted the essential feature of "the best" education. This view has undergone substantial change in the twenty-first century, reflected in the extended series of projects launched by MEXT over nearly a half-century.

The 2005 Report emphasized that this conception and construct of the university are premised on the underlying acceptance of the elite nature of the university, one which increasingly has failed to meet the requirements of a twenty-first-century population. In support of this critique, the 2005 Report explicitly cited José Ortega y Gasset's critique of the university in the 1930s Spain and the views of Clark Kerr in the United States in the 1960s to emphasize the point that universities should also have a social service role, as well as those focused on education and research.

Reforming Its Higher Education System for Regional Development

As stated above, the higher education policy of MEXT will convert from that of "making HE policies and restraints" to "offering and leading the future blueprint" for the twenty-first century. The focus of HE policy is changing from government regulation and planning to emphasizing competition among universities and evaluation by society. This shift was part and parcel of the 2006 revised Basic Act on Education emphasis on adding the "social contribution" mission to universities.

To contribute to this changing context, in June 2017 the National Universities Association issued an interim report entitled "The Future of National Universities in Higher Education." The report referenced other countries, including China and South Korea in East Asia, that have taken substantial measures to improve their HE achievement levels and increase their participation in the international competition for status and recognition in the current climate of globalization. For example, South Korea's POINT project divides its national universities into the categories of stronghold universities, regional central universities and special purpose universities. The developing functional differentiation of the national universities in Japan will also acknowledge the different functions and target arenas of these universities at multiple levels: global, national, and local. According to the same report, 66% of college students are concentrated in the Three Largest City Areas,[6] with 34% in other areas. A total of 31.6% of national universities are located in the Three Largest City Area, leaving 68.4% to be distributed throughout the remainder of the country. With a more even distribution of students and facilities, one policy goal is that 55 of the national universities will both commit to the development and economic revitalization of local enterprises as well as play an important role in regional development. The control of private universities in the development of the Tokyo Area will also help government strengthen local policy development.

Reforming Higher Education System for Global Competition

By the end of 2016, a total of 25 Japanese were home to faculty who had won Nobel Prizes, the achievements of which are widely viewed as evidence of the excellent educational and research ability of national universities. The many MEXT programs reviewed above are deemed of critical importance to continue the strengthening of university elites at the national level and to establish high-level education research bases underwritten by key financial support to succeed in further types of global competition. Within the same revised policy frame, national universities, especially, the designated 15 "excellent feature" universities will still play an important role in cultivating outstanding talent and achievements throughout the country. 74.1% of the enterprises surveyed for the MEXT reports indicated that a problem of "training and ensuring the domestic talents who promote the development of globalization" when setting up and running enterprises abroad (METI 2010). Cultivating talents to cope with global competition and revitalizing industrial development are also values and policy goals included in the Basic Plan for Promotion of Education II and a national development strategy entitled "Japan is Back" (MEXT 2014). Another report entitled, "The Future of National Universities in Higher Education," also emphasized that national universities have traditionally led HE development in Japan and will continue to constitute the core of Japanese HE. With the aforementioned persistent decline of the population of 18-year olds to an estimated less than 1 million by 2030, this core of 16 universities categorized as "world excellence" and 15 as having "excellent feature(s)" will become the stronghold of quality that will enable Japan to be a leader in cultivating domestic talents and promoting international exchanges on the world stage in a manner expected and required by the country's core business community.

ISSUES AND PROSPECTS: IMPLICATION OF THE REFORMS IN THE TWENTY-FIRST CENTURY

Rebuilding the New University Philosophy in the Twenty-First Century

The various projects mentioned above reflect the HE dimensions that the Japanese government, industry, and other related departments are seeking to explore in a systematic manner to prepare for the transition and emerging policy environment being created by changing globalization and the realities of Japan's demographic transformation. After more than ten years of such investigation and discourse, Japan has gradually formed its own road, even as some critical issues remain to be faced. Three are worthy of specific emphasis.

In 2006, the state emphasized regional contributions as the explicit third mission of universities and in so doing displaced the Humboldt classic idea of the university and did so by transforming the fundamental policy structure of public HEIs in Japan.

As a study by Nakatsuka and Odagiri in 2016 has documented, after 2006, universities and the local environments in which they resided undertook explicit efforts to promote cooperation. The law mandating such acts of cooperation specifies various types of such actions, including those focused on exchanges. The new position of the law is divided into the exchange type, the development value type, the solution of the subject type and the knowledge common ownership type based on determinations of their professional strength and weakness. State and local autonomy are also actively promoted within the structure of cooperation. It is important to note that when the central government has moved to redress what it has characterized as "related financial subsidies," some confusion has resulted over the precise intent of the outcomes that such efforts are meant to produce. For example, in 2017, MEXT started a project entitled "Program for Promoting Regional Revitalization by Universities as Centers of Community: COC+Program" (https://www.jsps.go.jp/j-coc/index.html). The ultimate goal of the project, as indicated above, is to address the demographic dilemma that the younger age population is overly concentrated in Tokyo. Thus, one of its outcome indicators is "the new employment rate and the number of new employment in the cooperative autonomous enterprises." From the viewpoint of making a "local contribution," some respondents lack clarity as to what would satisfy these criteria. Similar confusions exist about just what constitutes desired and successful outcomes for "implementing the university and regional cooperation matters." These have been summarized as constituting "local dissatisfaction and university unrest."

In January 2018, a report entitled "The Future of National Universities in Higher Education (Final Report)" was issued by The Japan Association of National Universities. This report defined regional cooperation as "providing a wide range of learning places for students through internships, so as to enable them to form a sense of occupation and entrepreneurship." The limits are very narrow. How to gradually turn "local contribution" into a real university's third mission in the future continues to be a challenging issue. At the same time, how to establish a socially recognized university philosophy and central idea that replaces the Humboldt concept of the university will continue to be challenges for Japan universities to face as the twenty-first century progresses.

Rebuilding Faculty Identity

In the twenty-first century, it is presumed that the nature and role of faculty members will also need to undergo change. Recently, faculty members within Japanese universities have increasingly become participants in the market economy. Before incorporation of the national universities in 2004, faculties had largely consisted of scholars comfortable in their attribution of ivory tower isolation for more than half a century; after the corporatization of national universities in 2004, faculty members "walked out of the academic ivory tower" (as it were) and into a new role as market participants. The MEXT report, "The Status and Issues of the National University after Its Corporatization (Intermediate Report)" (2010), indicated that after 2004, the amount of time available to faculty members for the education-transmission role of the classroom and for dedicated research had decreased, as had the number of published academic papers. There was no indication that the quality of academic papers had improved. It can be said that the expansion of the basic university philosophy to engage in an explicit social role has directly affected the identity of faculties and those who constitute them. The transformation from a role and identity of a single (and presumed relatively independent) scholar to "a scholar and a participant in market competition" has been a process of transformation from a single identity to one that is far more pluralistic and multifaceted. The process of transformation throughout the near future will be slow and with multiple challenges for those who continue to constitute the faculties of national universities under these demanding conditions of change.

Rebuilding New Balance Between Universities

It has been over 130 years since the founding of the imperial university in 1886. Following the Second World War, the reform of the school system led the government to establish a national university in every prefecture according to the principle of "one prefecture, one national university." Under the guidance of what was then the Ministry of Education, Japan's universities took the form of a pyramid, the apex of which was the University of Tokyo. National universities that formed, especially the seven imperial universities including the University of Tokyo, Kyoto University, Nagoya University, Tohoku University, Osaka University, Kyushu University, and Hokkaido University, have been clearly the most highly statused of the national universities and have had the role of promoting and achieving the highest levels of research in Japan. This institutional hierarchy continued up to the point of transformation signaled by the corporatization of national universities.

However, as a result of the introduction of the competitive dynamic that has been built into such transformations, two distinct changes have resulted. First, Kyushu University and Hokkaido University, both members of seven traditional imperial universities, failed to enter the list of "Designated National Universities" (2017–), a determination that requires the selected universities to be among the top ten in Japan in the three fields of "research," "social cooperation" and "international cooperation." Neither Kyushu University nor Hokkaido University could reach the standard established for inclusion for the status "international cooperation." This has had the effect of subverting the traditional "old empire university" title, which suggests that the identity of institutions included in the traditional attribution of the top class of Japanese universities could be rebuilt in the near future.

A further and clear implication is that when applying for the various competitive projects and funds mentioned above, those universities at the top of the resulting status pyramid are extremely powerful, with the result that in most competitions for resources, those further down in the status hierarchy cannot effectively compete. The result is that policies of long-term investment will tend to reinforce the gap between the top and bottom universities.

Implications of Twenty-First-Century Reforms

The twenty-first century for Japanese HE has witnessed its emersion into the realms of globalization and regionalization. As implied by the 2005 and 2017 MEXT Reports, the governmental aim has been to focus on providing financial support through specific projects, encouraging universities to bring to bear their own particular characteristics and strengths to improve their overall efficiency in response to the complex challenges brought by globalization and the declining birthrate, and their sense of social responsibilities to contribute to local economic development, and the revitalization of the country. These initiatives have brought profound changes to Japanese HE, which has become characterized by being replete with competition and challenge. In the twenty-first century, the traditional emphasis on harmony will be rebuilt in university culture, and the traditional atmosphere of education and research that persisted for more than half of the twentieth century will become a permanent memory.

NOTES

1. The corporatization of national universities is called the third university reform after the establishment of university in the Meiji Era (1868–1912) and the reform of school system in the Showa Era (1926–1989).
2. According to the National Institution for Academic Degrees and Quality Enhancement of Higher Education, CHE is a deliberative body within the former MEXT which discussed key issues on the enhancement of university education in response to the request of the minister. The council's responsibilities have now moved to the Subdivision on Universities of the CCE, in accordance with the restructuring of ministries in 2000. http://www.niad.ac.jp/.
3. The headquarters of Recreation of Town, People and Work was set up by the Cabinet Meeting in September 3, 2014.
4. For details, please refer to "National Universities", MEXT, http://www.mext.go.jp/en/about/relatedsites/title01/detail01/sdetail01/1375122.htm.

5. Tokyo Area includes Tokyo, Chiba Prefecture, Kanagawa Prefecture, and Saitama Prefecture. https://mainichi.jp/articles/20180120/k00/00m/010/143000c.
6. The Three Largest City Area includes Saitama, Chiba, Tokyo, Kanagawa, Aichi, Kyoto, Osaka, and Hyogo Prefecture.

REFERENCES

Mainichi Shinbun. 19 January 2018. The Freezing of Quotas in 23 Districts for Ten Years (*23 Ku Nai no Daigaku no 10 Nenkan Teiin Tōketsu*). Accessed February 1, 2018.

MEXT. 2005. On the Future of Higher Education in Japan. Available at: http://www.mext.go.jp/b_menu/shingi/chukyo/chukyo0/toushin/05013101.htm. Accessed July 14, 2017.

MEXT. 2010. The Status and Issues of the National Universities After Its Their Corporatization (Intermediate Report). Available at: www.mext.go.jp/a_menu/koutou/houjin/. Accessed July 30, 2017.

MEXT. 2014. On the Context of Young People Studying Abroad. Available at: https://www.cas.go.jp/jp/seisaku/ryuugaku/dai2/sidai.html. Accessed June 9, 2016.

MEXT. 2017. On the Future Conception of Higher Education in Japan. Available at: www.mext.go.jp/b_menu/shingi/gijyutu/. Accessed January 2, 2018.

MEXT. Annual Report on School Basic Survey.

Ministry of Economy, Trade and Industry (METI). 2010. A Questionnaire Survey on the Cultivating of Global Talents (*Gurōbaru Jinzai ni Kansuru Ankēto Chōsa*).

Nakatsuka, Masaya, and Tokumi Odagiri. 2016. Reality and Challenges in Community-University Partnership. *Journal of Association of Rural Planning* 35 (June, 1): 6–11.

Prime Minister of Japan and His Cabinet. 2013. Japan Is Back (*Nippon Saikō Senryaku*). Available at: https://www.kantei.go.jp/jp/singi/keizaisaisei/kettei.html. Accessed June 30, 2017.

Prime Minister of Japan and His Cabinet. 2014. Town, People, and Work (*Machi, Hito, Shigoto Sōsei*). Available at: https://www.kantei.go.jp/jp/headline/chihou_sousei/. Accessed May 30, 2017.

The Japan Association of National Universities. 2017. The Future of National Universities in Higher Education (Intermediate Report). Available at: http://www.janu.jp/news/teigen/20170615-wnew-teigen.html. Accessed January 3, 2018.

The Japan Association of National Universities. 2018. The Future of National Universities in Higher Education (Final Report). Available at: http://www.janu.jp/news/teigen/20180126-wnew-future-vision-filnal.html. Accessed March 1, 2018.

Ushiogi Morikazu. 2008. *Does the The Humboldt Philosophy End? The New Dimensions of Modern Universities.* Tōshindō.

CHAPTER 8

Changes to Internationalization of Japan's Higher Education? An Analysis of Main Findings from Two National Surveys in 2008 and 2017

Futao Huang

INTRODUCTION

Despite various interpretations of the phrase "internationalization of higher education," it is generally acknowledged that the internationalization of higher education (HE) has been playing a significant role in the emergence and development of Japan's HE. As early as the later nineteenth century when the Meiji government implemented a variety of policies to establish a modern HE system and pursue the modernization of Japanese society, relevant activities such as hiring foreign experts, academics and scholars, dispatching Japanese scholars and students to Western countries,

F. Huang (✉)
Research Institute for Higher Education,
Hiroshima University, Hiroshima, Japan
e-mail: futao@hiroshima-u.ac.jp

© The Author(s) 2019
D. E. Neubauer et al. (eds.), *Contesting Globalization and Internationalization of Higher Education*,
International and Development Education,
https://doi.org/10.1007/978-3-030-26230-3_8

and introducing Western norms, ideas, and practice to Japan by translating Western publications, etc., were carried out. As discussed in the next section, since the 1970s when the report concerning internationalization of Japan's education was published by the OECD more ambitious policies and national-level projects were developed by the Japanese government to facilitate the internationalization of HE (OECD 1971). As a result, more radical changes have occurred in the internationalization of Japan's HE compared with the previous phrases of HE development in the postwar period. This is especially true since the 1990s when influences from economic globalization, requests for enhancing the global competitiveness of Japan's HE, the market, a continual decline in numbers of the 18-year-old population in Japan, and the massification of HE have increasingly shaped such internationalization. Significant research has been conducted concerning the internationalization of Japan's HE focused on policy analysis, numbers of inbound international students, the internationalization of university curricula, international faculty at Japanese universities, and so forth. However, little research has been undertaken comparing changes that have occurred in the internationalization of Japanese universities at the institutional level which was viewed by institutional leaders in charge of internationalization or international affairs in Japanese universities based on national surveys with a similar questionnaire in recent years.

The purpose of this chapter is to discuss Japanese university leaders who valorize internationalization, and how their internationalization strategies have been influenced by the changing international context, including the above drivers from 2008 to 2017 in particular. By presenting relevant findings from two national surveys of institutional leaders who took major responsibility for the internationalization in Japanese universities and colleges, the study addresses whether any changes had occurred in their views of the internationalization imperative, important practices of internationalization, the international status of Japan's universities, and key factors which might have impacted changes to the internationalization of Japan's HE from a quantitative perspective. The chapter concludes by arguing that first, no radical changes occurred in the internationalization of Japan's universities from 2008 to 2017 despite impacts from globalization or other drivers; second, the internationalization of Japan's universities is ongoing and still highly valued despite these new circumstances; third, the internationalization of Japan's universities exhibits strong non-commercial characteristics; fourth, a majority of university leaders believe that the research productivity of Japan's universities has already reached

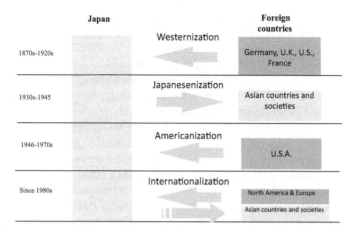

Fig. 8.1 Changing phases of internationalization of Japan's higher education (Created by author)

international standards; and finally, this study shows significant sectoral variation in attitudes and approaches to internationalization.

RESEARCH BACKGROUND

Figure 8.1 indicates the changing phases of the internationalization of Japan's HE since the late nineteenth century. Based on the relationship between Japan and foreign countries in the context of international activities, changes in the internationalization of Japan's HE can be practically divided into four phrases as follows:

In the first phase (late nineteenth century–late 1920s), as mentioned earlier, the impact of Western ideas and patterns on the formation of the Japanese modern HE system is evident and considerable. Earlier research suggests that:

All of the higher education systems considered here have Western roots and use basically Western models. In Asia, as in the rest of the world, the contemporary university is a basically Western institution, tracing their roots to the medieval European universities and shaped by the particular Western power that was the colonial ruler. In the case of Japan, China and Thailand,

foreign influences were chosen with independence, but the models were
foreign nonetheless. (Altbach and Selvaratnam 1989, p. xii)

At the time, as one way of learning from foreign ideas and patterns of HE,
foreign experts and scholars from different fields were invited to visit Japan.
For example, in 1876 alone, there were 78 foreign faculty members who
were involved in professional and language teaching activities, and in most
cases taught in languages other than Japanese (MOE 1992). According to
Ebuchi (1997), because Japan made huge efforts in learning from Western
countries and building a modern HE system based on France, the UK and
the USA, this period of internationalization of HE is also called "the phase
of Westernization."

   The second phase took place between 1930 and 1945. Especially since
the 1930s, academic activities in Japan were basically dominated by nationalism and militarism, except for a very few fields in medicine and engineering, Western academic standards, including the teaching of the English
language, were forbidden in Japan. Meanwhile, the Japanese educational
model and conventions were exported to Korea, Taiwan, and some South-
Asia countries as one control measure in the colonizing of these countries.
In contrast to the introduction of Western academic standards in the previous phase, by absolutely denying all the Western academic norms and
conventions, especially those of the U.K. and the U.S., Japan's HE during this period took primary form as exporting Japanese academic values
and standards to Asian countries and areas. Under the rigid regulation
and control of the central government, academic freedom and institutional
autonomy were greatly curtailed (Huang 2011).

   In the third phase (1946–1970), this period was characterized by the
dominant influences of the USA on almost every aspect of Japan's HE. After
WWII, impacted by US ideas imbued during its occupation of Japan, the
country restructured its national HE systems. For example, educational
subjects based on democracy replaced the former educational materials
closely relating to nationalism and militarism. Japan realized the massification of HE and the near-universal access to HE by building new national
and local public higher education institutions (HEIs) and encouraging the
expansion of private universities and junior colleges. During the process,
the numbers of female students greatly expanded.

   Throughout the fourth phase (late 1970–present), new and huge
changes could be identified in the internationalization of Japan's HE.
For example, one of the most remarkable changes in the 1980s was the

government's creation of a national policy of accepting 100,000 incoming international students by the early twenty-first century in 1983. In the 1990s, recent policies and strategies emphasized improving the international aspects and perspectives of individual HEIs and their ability to compete at an international level. In order to achieve these goals, individual academics were encouraged to provide more English-taught degree programs and attract more international students with demonstrations of high quality. Especially those working in leading research national universities were and are required to be more involved in international exchange activities and publish more articles or books internationally (Huang 2007). With the increased impacts from globalization in particular since the 1990s, increased numbers of private institutions have attempted to export their educational activities by providing transnational programs in other countries. For example, Waseda University, one of the top private universities in Japan, announced that in 2006 it would initiate a graduate school in co-operation with Nanyang Technological University in Singapore and offer a double Master of Business Administration (MBA) graduate program in technology management for students mostly coming from South-Asian countries. Upon successful completion of this program, students are awarded two master's degrees—an MBA from Nanyang Technological University and an MBA in technology management from Waseda University (Huang 2005).

Further, the Japanese government revised the legislation concerning the approval of foreign institutions in Japan and adopted new strategies for recognizing transnational branches and programs. For example, in February 2005, Japan's Ministry of Education, Culture, Sports, Science and Technology (MEXT) officially recognized Temple University Japan (TUJ), which is the oldest and largest American university in Japan. This approval makes it possible for Japanese universities to recognize and accept TUJ credits and allows TUJ graduates to apply to the graduate schools of Japanese public universities. In 2009, the government launched the "Global 30" program, aimed at accepting 300,000 foreign students by 2020. In order to achieve the goal, 13 universities, including 7 national and 6 private, were selected to play a central role in implementing the program. With additional funding from the central government, these universities are required to accept many more international students as well as to develop new English-taught degree programs.

In 2012, the Japanese government implemented the "Global Human Resources" project in order to foster Japanese university graduates with a global perspective, independent thinking skills, creativity and understanding of different cultural values, through industry, academia and governmental collaboration. The project consists of two types of participating institutions. Type A institutions are concerned with university-wide global human resources development. The project requires the selected universities to play a leading role in stimulating the globalization of other Japanese universities (MEXT 2012). In 2014, the Japanese government issued another national project: the "Top Global University Project." This project aims to enhance the international compatibility and competitiveness of HE in Japan. It provides intensive financial support for selected universities that are expected to press forward with comprehensive internationalization and university reform. Once more there are two types of institutions in the project. Type A (Top Type, 13 universities) is for world-class universities that have the potential to be ranked in the top 100 according to global university rankings. Type B (Global Traction Type, 24 universities) is for innovative universities that will continue to lead the internationalization of Japanese society, based on continuous improvement of their current internationalization efforts. It is reported that the central government will allocate 7.7 billion JPY annually for selected universities for 10 years (MEXT 2016).

The following reports on the relevant findings of two national surveys with a similar questionnaire in 2008 and 2017, and is focused on two distinct questions:

1. how Japanese university leaders have valorized the changes occurring in the internationalization of Japan's universities, and
2. the main characteristics of internationalization that Japan's universities have displayed.

In order to address these two questions, this chapter uses data from the two national surveys of vice presidents or institutional leaders in charge of internationalization. The two surveys were administered with a similar questionnaire. In the first survey, 765 questionnaires were sent to all potential respondents in December 2007. By March 2008, altogether 624 respondents (82.5% return rate) were received. In the second survey, 744 questionnaires were sent in March and by April 2017, with a total of 173 responses (23.3% return rate) received from respondents.

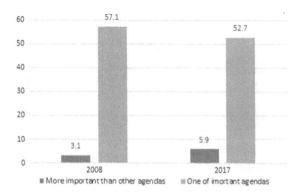

Fig. 8.2 Importance of internationalization among university-wide agendas % (Yonezawa, A. [2008]. Relevant data from survey of Japanese institutional leaders about evaluation on the internationalization of Japanese universities. Research Institute for Higher Education, Hiroshima University of Japan [2017]. Relevant data from survey of Japanese institutional leaders about facilitating the internationalization of Japanese universities)

Data Analysis and Main Findings

Figure 8.2 shows that although the proportion of those who agreed that internationalization is more important than other agendas declined from 57.1% in 2008 to 52.7% in 2017, no significant differences could be found in the responses to the importance of internationalization over the period. More importantly, more than half of the Japanese institutional leaders confirmed the importance of internationalization among their university-wide agendas.

In the two surveys, the goals of internationalization include enhancing the quality of research and faculty, stimulating the vigorousness of research activities, sending domestic faculty abroad, and improving the reputation of the university (Fig. 8.3). Among all these goals in 2008, it seems that Japanese institutional leaders considered enhancing the quality of research to be the most important goal (36.7%), followed by improving the quality of faculty (36.5%), stimulating vigorousness of research activities (33%), sending domestic faculty abroad (32.9%), and improving the reputations of their universities (32.7%). As of 2017, the largest number of respondents still thought that enhancing the quality of research to be the most important goal (34.3%), but improving the reputation of their universities became

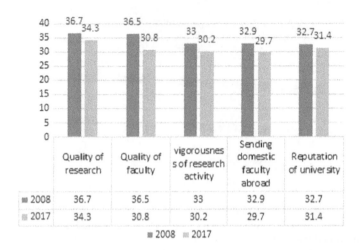

	Quality of research	Quality of faculty	vigorousness of research activity	Sending domestic faculty abroad	Reputation of university
2008	36.7	36.5	33	32.9	32.7
2017	34.3	30.8	30.2	29.7	31.4

■ 2008   ■ 2017

Fig. 8.3 Frequently cited goal of internationalization % (Yonezawa, A. [2008]. Relevant data from survey of Japanese institutional leaders about evaluation on the internationalization of Japanese universities. Research Institute for Higher Education, Hiroshima University of Japan [2017]. Relevant data from survey of Japanese institutional leaders about facilitating the internationalization of Japanese universities)

the second important goal (34.1%), followed by improving the quality of faculty (30.8%), stimulating the vigorousness of research activities (30.2%), and sending domestic faculty abroad (29.7%). On balance, although the proportions of responses to the frequently cited goals of internationalization decreased from 2008 to 2017, no significant differences could be found in their answers to the goals of internationalization over the period.

Figure 8.4 provides data on the international status of Japan's universities in terms of their research productivity, educational activities, and social service. Although the proportions of responses to all these three questions dropped from 2008 to 2017, no significant differences could be found in the responses to the international status of Japan's universities over the period. Noticeably, over half of Japanese institutional leaders believed that their research productivity has already reached international standards. In contrast, only 43.6 and 39.6% of them thought that the educational activities of Japan's universities had already reached international status in 2008 and 2017, respectively. As for the area of social service, only 40.7 and 32.6%

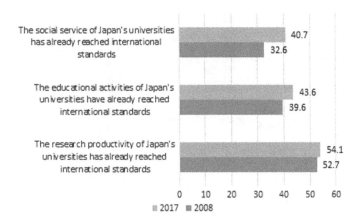

Fig. 8.4 International status of Japan's universities % (Yonezawa, A. [2008]. Relevant data from survey of Japanese institutional leaders about evaluation on the internationalization of Japanese universities. Research Institute for Higher Education, Hiroshima University of Japan [2017]. Relevant data from survey of Japanese institutional leaders about facilitating the internationalization of Japanese universities)

of them responded that Japan's universities have reached international status, respectively.

Detail concerning the important practices of internationalization in the institutions to which the respondents belong is provided in Fig. 8.5. In general, there were fewer respondents to this question in 2017 than those in 2008 due to fewer numbers of institutional leaders participating in the survey in the latter year. When asked to identify these practices, the top responses from all participants are outbound student mobility (543 persons), followed by hiring international faculty and researchers (534 persons), dispatching academic and administrative staff abroad (517 persons), strengthening student's English proficiency (515 persons), and accepting international students (417 persons) in 2008.

The largest numbers of the later responses suggest a similar pattern to that of 2008, namely, 163 of them believed that the outbound mobility of students was the most important practice in their institutions, but this was followed by strengthening student's English proficiency (153 persons), citing the same important practices of hiring international faculty and researchers (137 persons), dispatching academic and administrative

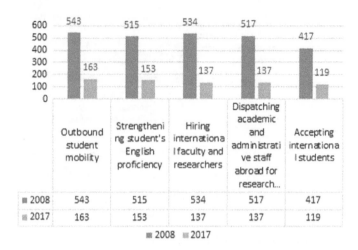

	Outbound student mobility	Strengtheni ng student's English proficiency	Hiring internationa l faculty and researchers	Dispatching academic and adm in istrati ve staff abroad for research...	Accepting internationa l students
■ 2008	543	515	534	517	417
■ 2017	163	153	137	137	119

■ 2008 ■ 2017

Fig. 8.5 When asked to identify important practices of internationalization, the top response from all respondents (person) (Yonezawa, A. [2008]. Relevant data from survey of Japanese institutional leaders about evaluation on the internationalization of Japanese universities. Research institute for higher education, Hiroshima University of Japan [2017]. Relevant data from survey of Japanese institutional leaders about facilitating the internationalization of Japanese universities)

staff abroad (137 persons), and accepting international students (117 persons) in 2017. Clearly, the biggest change in their responses is their providing second ranking to the hiring of international faculty and researchers in 2008, while in 2017 this status was given to strengthening students' English proficiency. One of the main reasons behind this shift has been the implementation of the "Global 13" project in 2009, the "Global Human Resources" project in 2012, and the "Top Global" project in 2014 in which Japanese universities, especially those which were selected as member universities of these projects and received relevant financial support from the government, have been required to develop and provide more English-taught degree programs for both international and domestic students.

Data suggesting that there were no significant differences in obtaining funding through internationalization-related activities between 2008 and 2017 are provided in Fig. 8.6. Over this period the largest numbers of respondents confirmed the obtaining of funding for international collaboration and research from external organizations (55.1 and 56.3%,

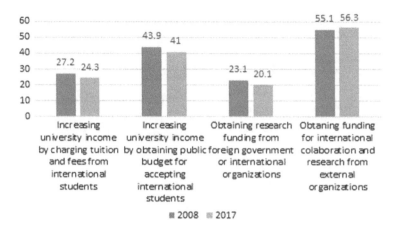

Fig. 8.6 Means of obtaining funding through internationalization-related activities % (Yonezawa, A. [2008]. Relevant data from survey of Japanese institutional leaders about evaluation on the internationalization of Japanese universities. Research institute for higher education, Hiroshima University of Japan [2017]. Relevant data from survey of Japanese institutional leaders about facilitating the internationalization of Japanese universities)

respectively), followed by the increase of university income from obtaining public budget support for accepting international students (43.9 and 41%, respectively), increasing university income by charging tuition and fees to international students (27.2 and 24.3%). These were followed by obtaining research funding from foreign governments or international organizations (23.1 and 20.1%, respectively), and increasing university income by charging tuition and fees from international students (27.2 and 24.3%, respectively). Importantly, more than half of Japanese institutional leaders emphasized the obtaining of funding for international collaboration and research from external organizations. Therefore, there is little doubt that Japan's internationalization is not motivated by accepting tuition and fees from international students, but mainly by obtaining revenues from external organizations.

Finally, Fig. 8.7 indicates the relationship between undertaking international activities and overall financial issues. Slightly different from previous findings, here significant differences could be found in this regard between 2008 and 2017. For example, in 2008 and 2017 the largest numbers of

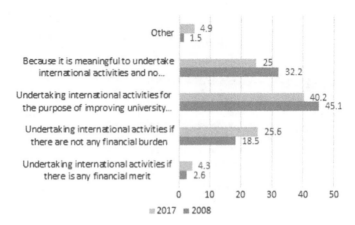

Fig. 8.7 Relationship between undertaking international activities and financial issues % (Yonezawa, A. [2008]. Relevant data from survey of Japanese institutional leaders about evaluation on the internationalization of Japanese universities. Research institute for higher education, Hiroshima University of Japan [2017]. Relevant data from survey of Japanese institutional leaders about facilitating the internationalization of Japanese universities)

respondents stressed undertaking international activities for the purpose of improving the university's image and for non-commercial aims (45.1 and 40.2%, respectively) in 2008, followed by undertaking international activities and expecting no economic outcomes (32.2 and 25%, respectively). Repeatedly, Japan's internationalization is not motivated by commercial purposes, but for enhancing the university image and for its own intrinsic sake.

In terms of the key drivers for changes that occurred in the internationalization of Japan's HE, it seems that several factors may explain the main findings from the two surveys (Huang 2017). First, although a large number of private universities needs to recruit sufficient numbers of fee-paying international students to maintain their operations, since the early 1970s, the central government has begun to provide public financial support to all private universities. For example, even as of 2010, public expenditure constituted more than 10% of the total revenues of private universities. Second, national universities have been expected to facilitate the advancement of basic and applied scientific research, some of which is on a large scale. A significant number of national universities remains more prestigious and are the centers of most graduate work at the Ph.D. level. Third, the influence from industry on Japan's internationalization cannot be overestimated for it has increasingly called for both government and universities to be more international, especially in the production of global human resources. Finally, increased academic competition worldwide has made Japan's universities realize the need to enhance their competitiveness through internationalization, particularly of teaching and research activities.

Conclusion and Discussion

As presented above, this study suggests the following findings:

- First, it appears that no radical changes occurred in the overall aspects of internationalization of Japan's universities from 2008 to 2017 despite various impacts from globalization or other external forces impacting on it. This implies that within the Japan HE structure, the nature of internationalization is relatively stable.
- Second, according to university leaders, the internationalization of Japan's universities is an ongoing process and still highly valued. There was not a clear or considerable transformation from internationalism to nationalism in Japan in 2008–2017, compared to those occurring in the USA and the UK.
- Third, the internationalization of Japan's universities is not primarily motivated by the market, evidence of which is that they continue to display strong non-commercial characteristics. The case study of Japan indicates that internationalization could be undertaken without necessarily being totally driven by neo-liberalism, entrepreneurism or the market in a specific time.

And finally, the majority of university leaders believe that the research productivity of Japan's universities has already reached international standards. Perhaps it is largely because a vast majority of Japanese faculty members show a strong preference in research and also allocate significant amounts of time in their research. This is especially true in the case of national universities in which research is more emphasized than either local public or private universities in Japan. Further, perhaps it is likely that each nation or system might have its own distinctive strength in internationalization.

REFERENCES

Altbach, P.G., and V. Selvaratnam (eds.). 1989. *From Dependence to Autonomy: The Development of Asian Universities*. Boston and London: Kluwer Academic Publishers.

Ebuchi, K. 1997. *Daigaku kokusaika no kenkyu* [Research in internationalization of university]. Tokyo: Tamagawa Press (in Japanese).

Huang, F. 2005. Internationalisation of the University Curriculum in Japan: Major Policies and Practice Since the 1980s. *Journal of Studies in International Education* 10 (2): 102–118.

Huang, F. 2007. Internationalisation of Higher Education in the Era of Globalisation: What Have Been Its Implications in China and Japan? *Higher Education Management and Policy* 19 (1): 35–50.

Huang, F. 2011. The Academic Profession in East Asia: Changes and Realities. In *The Changing Academic Profession in Asia: Contexts, Realities and Trends* (RIHE International Seminar Reports No. 17, pp. 113–131). Hiroshima: RIHE Hiroshima University.

Huang, F. 2017. How Do University Leaders View Internationalisation? *University World News*. 18 August Issue No 470.

MEXT. 2012. *Global jinzai ikusei suishin jigyou* [Promoting Global Human Resource project]. http://www.mext.go.jp/b_menu/houdou/24/09/attach/1326084.htm. Accessed October 25, 2016.

MEXT. 2016. *Statistical Abstract 2015 Edition*. Tokyo: National Printing Bureau.

MOE. 1992. *Gakusei hyakunijyuunenshi* [History of 120-Year School System] (pp. 39–40). Tokyo: Kabushiki kaisya gyousei (in Japanese).

OECD. 1971. *Review of National Policies for Education: Japan*. Paris: OECD.

CHAPTER 9

Excellence vs. Equity: How Taiwan Higher Education is Caught in a Trap for 'World Class' Status

Chuing Prudence Chou and Antonio Bolanos Casanova Jr.

INTRODUCTION

Since the 1980s, public investment in higher education (HE) has become increasingly linked to private actors and market forces rather than being allocated entirely by the state (Baker and Wiseman 2008). As previous research has shown (Roberts 2009; Chou et al. 2013; Connell 2013; Capano 2015; Rhoads et al. 2015), neoliberal economic ideology has made a significant impact on HE reform throughout the world. Taiwan has not been immune from experiencing these changes to its higher education institutions (HEIs).

The 1990s was a decade of significant transformation for Taiwan's economy and its effects on academia. This resulted in a significant expansion of HE with an increasing number of universities. By 2008, the number

C. P. Chou (✉) · A. B. Casanova Jr.
National Chengchi University, Taipei, Taiwan
e-mail: iaezcpc@nccu.edu.tw

© The Author(s) 2019
D. E. Neubauer et al. (eds.), *Contesting Globalization and Internationalization of Higher Education*,
International and Development Education,
https://doi.org/10.1007/978-3-030-26230-3_9

of university students surged to 1.12 million which was a 6.5-fold increase since 1984. Despite the surge in university students, public funding for HE in Taiwan decreased as the private sector and market forces were expected to play a more significant role in obtaining funding for HE. The drive for 'global excellence' in Taiwan meant that world-class university rankings were used to measure the extent that HEIs in Taiwan met this criterion. Additionally, this drive was utilized to boost national competitiveness and university visibility. Not only were universities in Taiwan competing among themselves, but also among other universities in the Asia-Pacific region and throughout other regions of the world.

In a global context, Taiwan's government has adopted policies rewarding institutions for increasing their international visibility and global competitiveness. These policies are often based on international citation indexes such as the Social Science Citation Index (SSCI), the Science Citation Index (SCI), and Engineering Index (EI). By rewarding scholars and universities in Taiwan with funding based on the number of research articles published in SSCI or SCI journals, Taiwan's government seeks to increase Taiwanese academia's international standing. As the internationalization of HE pits Taiwan against other institutions throughout the world, Taiwan seeks to become not only a source of international students, but also a prominent destination of international students.

In a local context, academic culture and research practices in the social sciences and humanities have been negatively affected as a result of the ranking systems used to measure the world-class status of HEIs. The pressure that Taiwanese scholars encounter to publish in internationally accredited journals and submit to evaluations has led to a backlash within the academic community against the government's HE policies. One result of the changes in HE policy has been the termination of scholars' employment from their institutions for failure to meet publishing quotas and/or failure to submit to university evaluations which they regard as unfair. In addition, the local perception of academics as 'public intellectuals' is gradually diminishing as the local relevance of research is being called into question. 'Global' is the predominant target for publication whether it be journals or readers. As a result of this, more publications are being written in English which is less accessible for local readers. A 'winner-takes-all' effect appears to dominate the local context of HE in Taiwan.

This chapter examines the effects of the pursuit of 'global excellence' and 'local equity' in Taiwan's HE. These effects include trends in relative publication growth and the number of papers published in Taiwan. Such trends are compared to other nations' respective trends to highlight Taiwan's pursuit of 'global excellence.' In addition, trends in SCI, SSCI, and EI paper publications, impact factors, and university rankings in Taiwan are further explored to understand the effects of pursuing 'global excellence.' Various cases will be presented to examine the academic community's disquiet over Taiwanese HE's pursuit of 'world-class status.' This disquiet within the academic community in Taiwan is a result of various consequences that have resulted from the extreme drive to pursue 'world-class status' in HE such as the gender gap and discrepancy, academic corruption, the SSCI Syndrome, and local impacts. The authors then conclude that benefits are not distributed evenly throughout academic fields, academic culture is shifting, latent anxiety between academic fields continues to grow, and the focus on meeting local needs is decreasing. Alternatives to the prevailing evaluation system of world-class universities advocated by HEIs and scholars are presented to remedy the issues that market-based education reforms have created (Chou 2014).

RELATIVE PUBLICATION GROWTH

In 1981, 543 academic papers were published in Taiwan, accounting for only 0.12% of global publications. This number has increased to more than 26,000 in 2012, consisting of 2.07% of global publications. Taiwan, along with South Korea, Mainland China, and Singapore, has seen the greatest relative growth in academic publications. In contrast, the USA and Japan maintained a relatively constant growth in academic publications (Kuo and Liu 2014). In addition, trends in the number of papers published show that Taiwan, as well as Singapore, South Korea, and India, is slowly rising. In contrast, Japan has slowed over the past decade, whereas Mainland China has significantly increased the number of papers its scholars have published. When the number of publications is compared to relative population in millions, Taiwan publishes 1131 papers per million people. This figure exceeds the publication to population ratio in South Korea, Japan, Mainland China, and even the USA. In addition, between 2008 and 2012, the publication growth rate in Taiwan was 18.29% which is significantly higher than the total birthrate of 1.21% (Reddit, n.d.; Kuo and Liu 2014).

SCI, SSCI, AND EI PAPER PUBLICATIONS

In Taiwan, policy reforms resulting from the impacts of globalization, neoliberal economic restructuring, and an increased emphasis on international competition have significantly affected HE. These policies, such as changes in governance, financing, evaluation, and salary structures, were intended to enhance academic quality. Currently, meritocracy, accountability, and networking among faculty and staff are now valued more in Taiwan's HE system than ever before (Chou 2018). As a result, the positive impacts anticipated by policymakers have not come to fruition and the emergence of a new phenomenon, the SSCI Syndrome, has grown rampant within Taiwan's system of HE (Chou 2014).

Today, individual scholars' research quality and impact are measured based on indicators from the following citation indexes: SSCI, SCI, EI, and so forth. These citation indexes were first owned by Thomas Reuters, a private, for-profit company located in the USA, and then was sold in 2016 (Reuters 2016). Major English-speaking universities in Australia, Canada, the USA, the UK, and New Zealand have long recognized their standards in order to quantitatively evaluate the research impact of their faculties.

Taiwan's Ministry of Education (MOE) constructed an evaluation system based on the use of quantitative indicators as a result of its pursuit of internationalizing HE. In 2003, the MOE implemented the use of international publication indicators as evaluation standards of academic performance (Chou 2014). Initially, this transition received widespread support from government officials in the MOE and the former National Science Council as well as academics, especially those in the natural sciences, economics, and other fields favoring the use of quantitative indicators. Although many supported the reforms, there was significant resistance within the academic community. In the same year as the evaluation standards of academic performance were reformed, academics began to organize in opposition to them (Chou 2014).

The rationale for using international publication indicators was based on an increasing emphasis on university internationalization in terms of public resource allocation and facilitation of HE reform policies to establish world-class universities. Universities have two primary driving factors in the pursuit of their world-class status. One is to maintain a superior position over other HEIS with respect to budgetary competition. The other factor is to make the university more attractive to prospective students and faculty.

Taiwanese HEIs expect to enhance their quality and competitiveness by promoting the use of international citation indexes as indicators for research performance. As a result of this development, Taiwanese HEIs have established administrative offices and centers devoted to the development of key subject areas and the promotion of 'quality' research. In order to evaluate performance, the actual number of faculty publications in the three databases is counted to determine the final ranking of each college and university. Therefore, academic faculty members are under significant pressure from both the government and their own institutions to publish internationally in order to obtain SSCI, SCI, and EI records for promotion and accreditation purposes (Ching 2014).

Impact Factors

Not only are the number and type of academic publications significant in measuring 'global excellence' in HE, but the impact factor of research articles published is also crucial in quantifying 'global excellence' which prioritizes research-related activities over less quantifiable academic endeavors. Citation indexes serve as a proxy for academic impact as it is a common assumption that research articles which are the most widely cited have made a greater contribution to their field than those that are less frequently cited. Yet, some research suggests there is strong evidence to doubt this assumption (Hazelkorn 2008; Ioannidis et al. 2007; Turner 2005). This indicates that there is a problem with relying solely on quantitative methods for measuring the 'impact' of research articles. Current measurements of 'impact' do not correspond to 'high-quality research' in today's publication-driven academia, especially when they do not correspond with the length of time necessary to conduct groundbreaking research and have it accepted as such (Chou and Cherry 2017). In addition, a lack of agreement exists over how much impact groundbreaking research has on the academic community. Unfortunately, new paradigms are not investigated early in their manifestation as pressure increases for academics to publish their work in citation index journals (Foster et al. 2015; Sarewitz 2016). Recent studies have also highlighted the fact that much research in science and engineering has been cited primarily by doctoral students instead of fellow researchers (Mohammadi et al. 2015). As a result, citation indexes favor 'safe' established research over groundbreaking research, which should raise doubts about their relevance as a measure of quality.

Despite such doubts regarding the reliability of impact measurement in determining the value of published research, Taiwan's impact factor has been on the rise over the past decade. From 2007 to 2011, Taiwan's impact factor was measured at 4.28; however, from 2011 to 2015, its impact factor increased to 5.31. In addition, Taiwan's reference count has increased during the same time period from 483,745 to 691,290 (MOST 2017; Kuo and Liu 2014). Therefore, the impact factor datum will remain a significant indicator used to evaluate academic performance in Taiwan's HEIs.

University Rankings

University rankings are another system of measurement used to quantify the quality of higher education in Taiwan. Within this system, Taiwan universities are pitted against themselves as well as other universities throughout the world. Demand for such data from students, employers, and academics has facilitated an increase in the use of international ranking data over the past two decades (Williams and Dyke 2004). The predominant criteria for ranking are based on the quantitative indicators of research output mentioned above. One example of this is in the widely cited, yet controversial, international ranking of universities published by Shanghai Jiao Tong University. The indicators of research quality, primarily articles published in the SCI Expanded and SSCI, have a weight of 20% (Docampo 2011). Thus, scholars tend to associate the 'best research' with the natural sciences and that indexed in SCI and SSCI, which may also place significant value on faculty with Nobel Prizes. Similarly, in 'Asia's Best Universities,' published by *Asia Week*, an important factor measured to determine research performance is citations in those academic journals tracked by the Journal Citation Index (Asia Week 2000). Citation data are also used in the *Times Higher Education* World University Rankings published in the UK, accounting for 30% of the overall score of an institution, and in the Quacarelli-Symonds (QS) rankings, accounting for 40% of the total score (Ching 2014). Therefore, university rankings are highly dependent on the presumptive 'best' research as determined by the amount of articles published, academic journals, predominantly natural sciences, and as valued in Citation Indexes.

Disquiet in the Academic Community

In the pursuit of 'global excellence' and 'local equity' in Taiwan HE, the academic community has responded to and challenged the status quo of quantifiable measurements used throughout the world to measure how 'international' universities have become. On the one hand, the academic community in Taiwan is not opposed to the internationalization of universities. On the other hand, the academic community has expressed grievances toward the way that this internationalization is measured. The methods used to quantify 'global excellence' are deemed insufficient and harmful to the role of local factors within academic standards and overall perceptions of academia.

Gender Gap and Disparities

One negative consequence of the drive for 'world-class' status and publication-focused HE research policies has been the widening of the gender gap and disparities within Taiwanese academia. The new reward system based on international journal publications has ultimately crippled the status of female faculty throughout the country since 2005 (Chou and Chan 2017). In particular, junior female faculty members in humanities and social sciences departments encounter significantly greater barriers to promotions and publication (Chou 2018). 'Elite' universities also tend to have greater gender disparities than 'non-elite' universities. Gender disparities are most visible when analyzing academic positions. Out of 162 total colleges and universities in Taiwan, only 14 were led by female presidents as of 2016 (Chou 2018). The percentage of female faculty at universities or colleges is increasing; however, the rate of increase is incredibly slow. For example, in 2007, female faculty accounted for 34.14% of total faculty; by 2014, female faculty accounted for only 35.21% of the total. This trend indicates that more can be done by Taiwanese HEIs and the Taiwan government to decrease the HE gender gap and disparity.

Corruption

The demonstrated bias in academic publication for quantitative presentations that significantly favors fields such as engineering and the natural sciences is reproduced within the Citation Indexes. In Taiwan, pressure on faculty to produce research articles in order to increase their institution's global competitiveness and 'global excellence' has resulted in numerous academic scandals, particularly in the Science, Technology, Engineering, and Mathematics (STEM) fields. The 'winner-takes-all' drive for 'excellence' has fostered corruption in the STEM fields as they seek to publish the most and as a result receive a far greater share of grant income. With significant financing at stake, academic fraud, peer-review process manipulation, and academic misconduct are more likely to occur as institutions scrap for as much funding as they can obtain. In recent years, numerous cases of academic misconduct and fraud committed by education ministers and faculty of prominent universities in Taiwan have shown that the current evaluating system of Taiwanese academia is taking its toll on the academic integrity of Taiwan's HEIs.

As a significant case in point, in 2014, the Minister of Education, at the time Chiang Wei-ling, resigned as a result of his alleged connection to an academic whose papers were retracted from an international journal because of suspected manipulation of the peer-review process (Wang et al. 2014). In 2017, two academic scandals occurred, one involving the President of National Taiwan University (NTU), at that time, and another involving a NTU faculty member. NTU President Yang Pan-chyr resigned after his term expired in June 2017 due to allegations of academic misconduct regarding a number of research papers he coauthored (Lin 2017b). During the early half of 2017, Professors Kuo Min-liang and Chang Cheng-chi of NTU were fired by the university after an investigation committee discovered that Kuo and his research team presented misleading images in six papers, two of which were retracted by science journals. Cheng was discovered to have improperly edited several images in four pages (Lin 2017a). Notably, these cases involved faculty in the physical sciences, which leads to questions over academic integrity within the whole range of physical sciences in Taiwan.

RESPONSES TO THE SSCI SYNDROME

Taiwan's MOE uses the number of SCI, SSCI, and EI paper publications that HEIs and scholars produce to measure global competitiveness and 'global excellence.' Universities in Taiwan often enforce publication quotas upon their faculty, a practice which has fostered a 'publish or perish' system of academic research. This has resulted in an 'SSCI Syndrome' in which SSCI publication is over-emphasized in the country's HE policy. Opposition from scholars of all disciplines to this high-pressure system has arisen as a result of the controversy aroused by a widely perceived over-emphasis on international publication. In particular, reactions from the humanities and social sciences, fields in which research accomplishments are greatly overlooked by the current publication drive, have been much stronger than other fields of study.

By 2003, academics had begun to organize in response to reforms that the MOE and NSC were attempting to push in order to establish new performance evaluation indicators (Chou 2014). Efforts by academics in the social sciences to increase the awareness of the potential negative impacts of using international publication indicators culminated in the publication of a text entitled: *Globalization and Knowledge Production: Reflections on Taiwan's Academic Evaluations* (Reflections Meeting Working Group 2004). Ultimately, these early efforts in altering the course of state-led reform proved unsuccessful.

As research has become more publication dominant, debates have raged on regarding the true nature of educational policies' performance indicators. There are significant questions as to whether these indicators overly emphasize global standards and whether these benchmarks are dominated by Western, predominantly American, traditions and practice (Mok and Tan 2004; Lai 2004; Wang 2014). In addition, given that English is a foreign language to the vast majority of researchers in Taiwan, they must strive to overcome greater linguistic obstacles than researchers from English-speaking countries or other societies with historically higher levels of English proficiency. Studies have indicated that often times the global norm of English as a *lingua franca* tends to ignore voices from the periphery, or non-English-speaking, world (Liu 2014).

Unfortunately, faculty members are increasingly falling victim to the SSCI Syndrome and the competitive winner-takes-all reward system that emphasizes research to the detriment of teaching and other academic contributions to society. Failure to meet research requirements of HEIs or a refusal to submit to an evaluation within Taiwan often leads to termination for faculty members. This has been the case even for faculty members who have earned teaching awards from prestigious national universities in Taiwan (Wang 2010).

Taiwanese university faculty members have taken the initiative to increase public awareness of debates over SSCI-related issues in HE. In November 2010, Taiwanese university faculty initiated an online petition calling for collective action. The petition had two purposes: first, to demand that Taiwan's government discontinue its policies of relying on indexed journals as primary indicators for university evaluation and funding and adopt alternative evaluation policies. Secondly, the petition urged public funding agencies to expand the quantity and variety of academic journals in the international and domestic journal citation databases and give equal weight to publications in the humanities and social sciences (Chou et al. 2013).

Since November 2010, the petition has attained support from academics and civil society. It has been endorsed by more than 3000 petitioners, 85% of whom are affiliated with the humanities and social sciences, while 10% are from science-related fields. In addition, the debates over SSCI have continued to attract public awareness, even national news coverage. In mid-2012, top government officials in Taiwan responsible for HE policy agreed to conduct an unprecedented review of the SSCI issue. Subsequently, the government made revisions to its SSCI funding policies and evaluation guidelines (NCCU Teachers' Association 2012). However, these minor policy changes merely address a portion of the demands of academics while the SSCI Syndrome remains a prominent feature within the overall structure and reward system of Taiwanese academia.

CONCLUSION

HE in Taiwan constantly faces challenges internationally and domestically which are exacerbated by the current evaluation system of universities and the continued integration of the private sector and market forces within overall university funding. Increasing pressure on Taiwanese HE faculty to 'publish or perish' has led to a corresponding frequency of serious academic scandals, an enlarging gender gap and disparity within HEIs, and the threat of academic corruption. The emphasis on university rankings, the number of internationally accredited publications, and the impact factor of research conducted by faculty at colleges and universities appears to have a variety of effects that have not proved to be beneficial to Taiwan's HE. Despite faculty publishing more papers than ever before, there is significant reason to doubt what sort of 'quality' is being produced and whether this contributes positively to making Taiwanese HEIs obtain 'world-class' status.

Resistance and criticism from Taiwanese college and university faculty members who view the current system as unfavorable to producing 'world-class' status HEIs has materialized significantly within the past decade, however, it remains to be seen how effective these scholars can be at successfully promoting alternatives for the Taiwan government to utilize in evaluating these institutions. Further research is necessary to understand what alternatives are available for HEIs in Taiwan and how faculty members of these institutions can implement these alternatives to make Taiwan competitive in the growing market of international education. For Taiwan, its competitiveness in global education as well as domestic education depends upon what policies are implemented and how effective they are at increasing Taiwanese HEI's competitiveness. From the research conducted, it is obvious that Taiwanese faculty members face an uphill battle in reforming their educational evaluation system. The SSCI Syndrome maintains a strong influence over Taiwan's HE policy making and institutions. It will ultimately take a collective effort from faculty, colleges and universities, and the Taiwan government to reform HE in Taiwan to be syndrome free. Such a system is not impossible to visualize, as it existed in the past, but there must be a collective desire to develop such a system in the present.

REFERENCES

Asia Week. 2000. Asia's Best Universities 2000. CNN. Retrieved from http://edition.cnn.com/ASIANOW/asiaweek/features/universities2000/index.html.

Baker, D.P., and A.W. Wiseman. 2008. Preface. In *The Worldwide Transformation of Higher Education*, ix–xii. Bingley, UK: Emerald.

Capano, G. 2015. Federal Dynamics of Changing Governance Arrangements in Education: A Comparative Perspective on Australia, Canada and Germany. *Journal of Comparative Policy Analysis: Research and Practice* 17 (4): 322–341.

Ching, G.S. 2014. ISI Perceptions and Hard Facts: An Empirical Study from Taiwan. In *The SSCI Syndrome in Higher Education: A Local or Global Phenomenon*, ed. C.P. Chou. Rotterdam, The Netherlands: Sense Publishers.

Chou, C.P. 2014. The SSCI Syndrome in Taiwan's Academia. *Education Policy Analysis Archives* 22 (29). http://dx.doi.org/10.14507/epaa.v22n29.2014.

Chou, C.P. 2018. University Governance and Leadership in Taiwan: An Empirical Study of the University President Profile. Paper presented at "A Comparative Study of University Governance, Institutional Leaders and Leadership in East Asia," 24 February, Garden Palace, Hiroshima, Japan.

Chou, C.P., and C.F. Chan. 2017. Governance and Academic Culture in Higher Education: Under the Influence of the SSCI Syndrome. *Journal of International and Comparative Education* 6 (2): 63–75.

Chou, C.P., and B. Cherry. 2017. Caught in a Trap: Impact Factors and the Scramble for "World Class" Status. *US-China Foreign Language* 15 (6): 404–408. https://doi.org/10.17265/1539-8080/2017.06.006.

Chou, C.P., H.F. Lin, and Y.J. Chiu. 2013. The Impact of SSCI and SCI on Taiwan's Academy: An Outcry for Fair Play. *Asia Pacific Education Review* 14: 23–31. https://doi.org/10.1007/s12564-013-9245-1.

Connell, R. 2013. The Neoliberal Cascade and Education: An Essay on the Market Agenda and Its Consequences. *Critical Studies in Education* 54 (2): 99–122.

Docampo, D. 2011. On Using the Shanghai Ranking to Assess the Research Performance of University Systems. *Scientometrics* 86 (1): 77–92. https://doi.org/10.1007/s11192-010-0280-y.

Foster, J.G., A. Rzhetsky, and J.A. Evans. 2015. Tradition and Innovation in Scientists' Research Strategies. *American Sociological Review* 80 (5): 875–908.

Hazelkorn, E. 2008. Learning to Live with League Tables and Ranking: The Experience of Institutional Leaders. *Higher Education Policy* 21: 193–215.

Ioannidis, J., N. Patsopoulos, F. Kavvoura, A. Tatsioni, E. Evangelou, I. Kouri, D. Contopoulos-Ioannidis, and G. Liberopoulos. 2007. International Ranking Systems for Universities and Institutions: A Critical Appraisal. *BMC Medicine* 5: 30–39.

Kuo, Y.F., and H.Y. Liu. 2014. An Analysis of Taiwan's Overall Academic Capacity. ResearchPortal. Retrieved from https://portal.stpi.narl.org.tw/index/article/28.

Lai, D.M. 2004. Quantitative Indexes Are Not the Panacea of Academic Evaluation (in Chinese). Paper presented at the Reflecting on Taiwan's Higher Education Academic Evaluation Conference, International Plenary Hall, National Library, Taipei, Taiwan.

Lin, S. 2017a. NTU to Fire Two Professors Accused of Academic Fraud. *Taipei Times*, February 16. Retrieved from http://www.taipeitimes.com/News/front/archives/2017/02/26/2003665722.

Lin, S. 2017b. NTU President to Resign Amid Scandal. *Taipei Times*, March 19. Retrieved from http://www.taipeitimes.com/News/front/archives/2017/03/19/2003667044.

Liu, Y.-J. 2014. Problems, Strategies, and Impact of SSCI Publication in English: Perceptions and Negotiations of Taiwanese Researchers. In *The SSCI Syndrome in Higher Education: A Local or Global Phenomenon*, ed. C.P. Chou. Rotterdam, The Netherlands: Sense Publishers.

Ministry of Science and Technology (MOST). 2017. The Impact Factors of SCI Papers in ROC (Taiwan). Retrieved from http://stats.moe.gov.tw/files/important/OVERVIEW_Y10.pdf.

Mohammadi, E., M. Thelwall, S. Haustein, and V. Larivière. 2015. Who Reads Research Articles? An Altmetrics Analysis of Mendeley User Categories. *Journal of the Association for Information Science and Technology* 66 (9): 1832–1846.

Mok, K.H., and J. Tan. 2004. Globalization and Marketization in Education: A Comparative Analysis of Hong Kong and Singapore. Cheltenham, UK: Edward Elgar. Retrieved from http://www.ireg-observatory.org/pdf/abstracts_and_speakers.pdf.

NCCU Teachers' Association. 2012. Petition Statement: Taiwan Competitiveness Forum. Retrieved from http://memo.cgu.edu.tw/yun-ju/CGUWeb/NCCUEdu2010/HomeAgainstSSCI.htm.

Reddit. n.d. Top 40 Countries by the Number of Scientific Papers Published. Retrieved from https://www.reddit.com/r/dataisbeautiful/comments/20k5dk/top_40_countries_by_the_number_of_scientific/.

Reflections Meeting Working Group. 2004. Globalization and Knowledge Production: Reflections on Taiwan's Academic Evaluations. *Taiwan Society Research Forum* 4. Retrieved from http://taishe.shu.edu.tw/book_forum_04.html.

Reuters. 2016. Thomson Reuters Announces Definitive Agreement to Sell Its Intellectual Property & Science Business to Onex and Baring Asia for $3.55 Billion. Reuters. Retrieved from https://www.thomsonreuters.com/en/press-releases/2016/july/thomson-reuters-announces-definitive-agreement-to-sell-its-intellectual-property-science-business.html.

Rhoads, R.A., C.A. Torres, and A. Brewster. 2015. Neoliberalism, Globalisation, and Latin American Higher Education. In *Second International Handbook on Globalisation, Education and Policy Research*, ed. Z. Joseph, 203–217. Dordrecht: Springer.

Roberts, P. 2009. A New Patriotism? Neoliberalism, Citizenship and Tertiary Education in New Zealand. *Educational Philosophy and Theory* 41 (4): 410–423.

Sarewitz, D. 2016. The Pressure to Publish Pushes Down Quality. *Nature* 533: 147. https://doi.org/10.1038/533147a.

Turner, D.A. 2005. Benchmarking in Universities: League Tables Revisited. *Oxford Review of Education* 31 (3): 353–371.

Wang, W.-L. 2010. It Is About Time for University Faculty to Be Alert Thanks to the Strict Evaluation System. *United News*. Retrieved from http://mag.udn.com/mag/campus/storypage.jsp?f_ART_ID=279045.

Wang, H.H. 2014. The Political Economy of Quantitative Indexes for Measuring Academic Performance. In *The SSCI Syndrome in Higher Education: A Local or Global Phenomenon*, ed. C.P. Chou. Rotterdam, The Netherlands: Sense Publishers.

Wang, C., D. Baker, and AFP. 2014. Education Minister Resigns over Scandal. *Taipei Times*, July 15. Retrieved from http://www.taipeitimes.com/News/front/archives/2014/07/15/2003595132/2.

Williams, R., and N.V. Dyke. 2004. The International Standing of Australian Universities. Melbourne Institute. Retrieved from http://www.melbourneinstitute.com/downloads/reports/ExecSumm.pdf.

CHAPTER 10

How 'Internationalism' and 'Nationalism' Get Along in Higher Education: A Thai Provincial University's Perspectives

Sudakarn Patamadilok

WHAT MAKES US COME THIS FAR?

To some world historians, a 'globalization big bang' is not considered as a *nouvelle* phenomenon given that the world in many ways has been 'globalized' since the 1490s through trade and markets (O'Rourke and Williamson 2002). Some scholars believe that such a bang was widely experienced following the 1820s through an increase in the complexity of trading expansion worldwide. In other views, the first era of globalization started in the late nineteenth century as a result of the British Empire's free trade zone, followed by the second era with the rise of transnational supply chains through a new kind of international order supported by the United States, and yet a subsequent third era with the intensification of regional powers throughout the world such as China, Nigeria, Brazil, with the more recent

S. Patamadilok (✉)
Kasetsart University, Bangkok, Thailand
e-mail: sudakarnp@nu.ac.th

© The Author(s) 2019
D. E. Neubauer et al. (eds.), *Contesting Globalization and Internationalization of Higher Education*,
International and Development Education,
https://doi.org/10.1007/978-3-030-26230-3_10

rapid growth of their economies (Hendrix 2012). These movements have been continually conceptualized, defined, and developed since the beginning of the twenty-first century. According to Pieterse (2012), contemporary globalization has been defined by three major changes: The emergence of new industrializing countries in the Global South which have become part of the world economy's leaders; development agencies that migrated from urban institutions to developing countries; and free-market forces that migrated toward growing state coordination.

Taking those views, it would seem as if globalization was only initiated and framed by economic matters. In reality as is widely accepted, it is a multidimensional process 'driven by technological innovation that effectuates social change and economic development by transforming a country into a modernized industrial, or developed nation,' reflected in the Human Development Index in terms of 'a country's population's life expectancy, knowledge and education measured by adult literacy, and income' (Pologeorgis 2017). This process can be perceived both as making the world 'a better place' (O'Neil 2017) and as 'under attack' (Broad 2016), depending on how we apply it in our varied contexts. In one sense, the trend creates a new form of living through a blend and exchange of knowledge, information, culture, tradition, and lifestyle. On the other hand, it seems to detach a sense and pride of identity, locality, uniqueness, and originality away from one's own life. These pros and cons have been repeatedly discussed in the decades that define contemporary globalization (Collins 2015).

While people around the world are gradually adopting various global dimensions into their lives, higher education (HE) as an intrinsic part of global activities is inevitably affected by a transformative international and national atmosphere in terms of language education (Kubota 2002), the knowledge society (Alvesson and Benner 2016) or education policy and practice (Grapragasem et al. 2014, p. 89). Many acts, policies, concepts, methods, activities, materials, and organizations within academia have been reformed and reset to serve such a global change. It is best, however, that this transformation is carefully approached and accomplished, as any substantive educational change usually influences both current and future generations. Not surprising therefore, various debates over the future and preferred courses for HE have emerged since the beginning of the millennium. As Delanty (2004, p. 241) argues, a university can turn into 'an anachronistic institution clinging to a modernity in ruins' if the world is not mindful of a collision between culture and technology which has become an important part of the context of contemporary higher education institutions (HEIs).

For Scott (2000), the impact of globalization is most evident along two important dimensions: First, globalization cannot be seen simply as a form of internationalism, but rather is better viewed within a complex diversity of nationalism(s); second, globalization marks a shift from modernity to postmodernity in terms of concepts and mentalities, a reality that directly influences universities caught in the midst of their own transformations.

The concern of these scholars is similarly focused on the question of how universities can survive in this rapidly changing environment. This has been exemplified at one level with the emergence of the Partnership for 21st Century Learning's (P21) renowned Framework for 21st Century Learning, which has had significant impact on teaching and learning worldwide at all levels in terms of framing the necessary skills and knowledge that learners will require to succeed in work and life (Partnership for 21st Century Learning 2007). Whereas the framework is perhaps most employed by institutions in the United States, it has been expanded on and adopted by other countries while being heralded as the desired focus for learning in the twenty-first century. One well-known example, the Ngee Ann Secondary School in Singapore, one of the country's seven Future Schools, applies technology and digital media in the classroom to enhance students' learning motivations via the Internet and social media (Edutopia 2012). Within this framework, the teacher no longer acts as a one-way knowledge-giver, but gives students an opportunity to access knowledge from various channels such as the Internet or social media apart from guiding and supporting them to analyze and synthesize data for their best application in the future (Boonpen 2015). In another example drawn from within HE, Nanyang Technological University of Singapore has changed its entire academic system to prepare graduates for the twenty-first-century workplace by creating knowledge to meet various global changes and develop innovative and responsible leaders for the future of Singapore, Asia, and the world (Kong 2014). This determined transformation seeks to move the university forward through a framework of four 'External Drivers':

1. **Global Environment** (Changing Economic, Landscape, Technological, Advancements, Challenges to Sustainability and Global Interdependence)
2. **Social Transformation** (Speed & Scale of Change, Cultural Diversity, Social Media, Social Inclusiveness and New Moral Dilemmas)

3. **Twenty-First-Century Skills** (Interpersonal Skills, Collaborative Skills, Thinking Skills, Communication Skills, Disciplinary Depth, Interdisciplinary problem-solving and Professional Integrity)
4. **EPIC Learners** (Experiential Participatory, Image driven and Connected)

The efforts of Nanyang Technological University have been rewarded as it has been ranked the No. 1 university in the world according to QS's Top 50 Under 50 years of age (2016–2017), the 11th in the world in the QS World University Rankings 2018, and 3rd in the QS University Rankings in Asia 2016 (Quacquarelli Symonds 2018a).

Highlighted by the examples of Singapore and most other countries, Thailand has also been influenced by these macro-global changes and the challenges they present. With respect to HE numerous legislative reforms, policies and regulations have been promulgated to cope with the effects of globalization in the country since the 1990s. Lauhathiansind and Chunbundit (2016, pp. 511–530) point to the change within academic systems brought on by the National Education Reform 1999 that focused on HE administration, personnel and financial management; the long-range plan for HE (2008–2022) that focuses on the quality of students, lifelong learning and employability of graduates in basic and vocational education with the ultimate aims to strengthen governance and accountability, to enhance staff development, to develop learning infrastructure, to promote institutional networking, to enhance national competitiveness, and to solve social issues; and the revision of the Private HE Institution Act which focuses on the quality and standards of private institutes.

Nonetheless, it should be pointed out that these developments have been mainly processed within the regional arena or ASEAN Community, not on global ground. Even though 'international programs,' which apply English as the instructive medium have been extensively offered in several public and private universities in Thailand, internationalization specifically built within HE systems has not been assured because the primary emphasis on the part of universities to generate fee income is the underlying rationale for such programs, which in large measure serve only particular and privileged groups (Lavankura 2013, p. 663). Chalapati's research on *The Internationalisation of Higher Education in Thailand* (2007) adds confirmation to this assertion with her finding that, since the 1990s, successive Thai governments have tried to build a globally skilled workforce through English-medium business graduate programs branded as 'international' at leading universities in Bangkok without considering the English proficiency of students passing through the programs or giving a clear idea of what internationalization means in the Thai context.

With respect to the international standing of Thai universities viewed through the lens of university rankings, only eight appear in the QS World University Rankings 2018 (Quacquarelli Symonds 2018d) namely: Chulalongkorn University (245th), Mahidol University (334th), Chiang Mai University (551st), Thammasat University (601st with a 4-star rating), Kasetsart University (751st), Khon Kaen University (801st), King Mongkut's University of Technology Thonburi (801st) and Prince of Songkla University (801st). The other 453 Thai HE institutions (Thai Association of Governing Boards of Universities and Colleges 2018) have blurry positions with respect to comparisons outside of Thailand. It is important to note that five of the rated universities are located in Bangkok, and all the eight HEIs regarded as leading Thai universities were established between 50 and 100 years ago. Due to their long history and respectful experience, it is not surprising that they are in the QS World University Rankings, but it raises the question of the relative status of the remaining Thai universities. Having not achieved world rankings or having no international courses to offer raises the issue of whether such institutions have no demonstrable value or if they are unable to maintain a suitable presence within the global higher education environment.

In this case, the question is raised within Thailand as to whether Thai HEIs should go further and drop a pin on achieving a certain destination because the world appears to be moving faster than the country's speed limit as set and controlled by the national policy which requires them to urgently support global economic movements and dynamic domestic socioeconomic forces. On the other hand, would it be perhaps a better and more prudent course for Thai HEIs to slow down their rates of change and pursuit of global goals and contemplate making full use of local wisdom, knowledge-and-skill preparation, and the domestic demographic context? By so doing, it is better assured that people can achieve recognized capabilities of full value within a domestic context before jumping into the global race. *To be or not to be international, that is the question.* This is the controversial issue which this chapter aims to consider, analyze, and discuss throughout from a Thai perspective.

Two Polarities: Internationalism and Nationalism in HE

Conflict, disagreement, and confusion are normal occurrences when two polarities meet such as the often cited issues of black and white, east and west, rich and poor, man and woman, human and animal, art and science, good and bad (Balabanis et al. 2001). This does not exclude the case of nationalism and internationalism in HE which has revealed a very similar dynamic when globalization has stepped into this territory. Taking Japan as an example, the internationalization movement known as *kokusaika* introduced just such an ambiguity into the country's education system before the end of the twentieth century. It had the consequence of inducing people to get caught up in the idea of resisting global currents and by so doing overlooking the value of fundamental changes essential for internationalism to proceed (Lincicome 1993). After analyzing questionnaires completed by Hong Kong and Mainland university students, Fairbrother (2003, p. 605) found that the emphasis on patriotic education in Mainland China and that of depoliticizing civic education in colonial Hong Kong influenced students' 'perceptions of political socialization, critical thinking dispositions, and national attitudes.' The reason why these two ideas have been conceived as opposites is simple: When globalization has moved in, a duel results between nationalists' sense of loss and internationalists' sense of pride and gain (Abdulsattar 2013).

From other perspectives, such a contestation's outcome is not always negative, but has been both positive and productive to HEIs in many countries. Starting from the international side, Singapore is a good example that displays an ability to adopt globalization thoughtfully and adjust it to HEIs in a very positive manner. Likewise, Malaysia has developed an understanding of globalization, embraced an instructive methodology, and focused on creating a knowledge-based society through the pursuit of four elements: employability, quality assurance, academia, and English language in order to catch up with the perceived international movement (Grapragasem et al. 2014). Their success is revealed in the country's Vision 2020 which aims to transform Malaysia into a fully developed nation in the near future. Regarding the bright side of nationalism, Wende and Zhu (2015) emphasize that China is establishing the world's largest HE system largely by following successful Western (mostly Unites States) models and good practices with 'creative adaptation' and 'Chinese characteristic.'

Within this modality, the creative adaptation component is comprised of:

1. **New Challenges and Persistent Concerns** focused on quality, graduate unemployment, inequality, academic freedom and institutional autonomy.
2. **Policy Paradoxes** such as sending students and faculty abroad, slowing down the reform for modern teaching and learning approaches, conserving national heritage and educational sovereignty against global threats.

Whereas the Chinese characteristic involves:

1. Global Public Goods and Soft Power
2. Chinese Diaspora
3. Confucius Institutes
4. Shanghai Ranking and the World-Class University Movement
5. China's New Silk Route: A New Epistemic Route.

From this nationalist standpoint, China is viewed as not just as a follower, but also a global leader in HE. To reach the goal, Wende and Zhu emphasize that the country requires a world-class system to be applied in HEIs to meet global demands with a strong mission and many possibilities for students by focusing on differentiation, deregulation, autonomy, and accountability. However, in many countries, especially developing ones, it seems that the polarities of internationalism and nationalism persist in HE. To understand the HE polarity phenomenon, the following charts might be helpful.

As suggested by Fig. 10.1, when internationalism moves in, nationalism embraces and transfers its impacts to HE in the form of policy. If the embrace and transformation are adjusted to suit local HEIs, every process and activity should get along well and make great progress within this context. As IMHE-Info states (OECD 2009, p. 3), the 35 member countries of OECD (i.e., all are Western, except Japan) have successfully co-operated and worked among each other by enhancing the role of HEIs through the 'economic, social and cultural development of their cities and regions.' On the other hand, if such enhancement does not happen, the international movement will simply make the national HE stay far away from where it

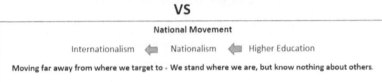

Fig. 10.1 International movement in higher education vs National movement in higher education

stands, often causing local people to forget their own identity and suffer a sense of loss (Hazelkorn 2015).

In Fig. 10.1, the consequence is suggested the other way round when taking national movement as a primary concern. Here, the HEI holds firmly to its national policy and tries to assert it into an international context. The conflict arises as the world is becoming more globalized, but the local HEI insists on standing alone, that is, not seeking in a purposive way to deal with the implications of globalization. This willingness to be ignorant of such profound changes isolates HE; people prefer to live within their closed territory and as a consequence know relatively little about the outside world.

Stated in this way, these two polarities probably appear exaggerated or framed within hyperbole, but such positions with regard to internationalization and globalization have actually occurred and played an important part in the development of HEIs worldwide as discussed in the following section.

A GLOBAL EFFECT TO A BUTTERFLY

In the age of globalization, it seems that most HEIs have geared themselves to be 'inter' through the adoption of or reference to different kinds of global standards such as the QS World University Rankings, world-class excellence awards, SCOPUS/SPRINGER journals, international conferences, English programs, or similar activities. HEIs which have greater capacity and support in terms of policy, budget, curriculum, materials, teaching staff, and learners' competence are able to move forward in adopting changes consistent with their goals with considerable speed. Their achievement in moving toward a globalized status is revealed in a considerable variety of Western countries such as Australia, Canada, Finland, France, the Netherlands, Sweden, Switzerland, the UK, the United States, and several Asian countries such as China, Japan, Singapore, South Korea, Taiwan, and including the autonomous territory Hong Kong, where their HEIs are well regarded within the 100 top universities in the world (Quacquarelli Symonds 2018c). Looking at these Asian HEIs closely, it can be seen that all of them have no problem in communicating in English even though it is not their mother tongue. There is no need to mention what positive or negative history has brought them into this advantaged state and made them able to step into a globalization modality relatively easily and manage to respond effectively to continuous global changes. Today, those countries have proved that they can take action seriously in developing a curriculum and overall academic environment that supports internationalism.

Thailand is an ASEAN country that has followed the trend of globalization. The action is clearly seen from national policies launched by successive Thai governments (Chalapati 2007) and recent actions announced by the government of Prime Minister Prayuth Chan-ocha: 'Thailand 4.0' (Secretariat of the House of Representatives, E-Library 2017) and the 'New-Breed Graduate Programs' initiative (Ministry of Education, National Education Information System 2018). Thailand 4.0 operating under the 'New Growth Engine' concept is an economic development model expanded from past models that emphasized Agriculture (Thailand 1.0), Light Industry (Thailand 2.0) and Advanced Industry (Thailand 3.0), which aim to unlock what have been referred to as the middle income trap, an inequality trap, and an imbalanced growth trap by promoting four main objectives: economic prosperity, social well-being, raising human values, and embracing environmental protection (Royal Thai Embassy 2018). In terms of education, Thailand 4.0 focuses on producing graduates with globally relevant knowledge and skills across all careers, especially those in industry, science and technology, through the promotion of innovation, creativity, research and technology (National Science and Technology Capability 2017).

In line with Thailand 4.0, the New-Breed Graduate Programs' mission is to cope with globalization within the academic context. As revealed by Clinical Professor Udom Kachintorn, the Deputy Minister of Education (Ministry of Education, National Education Information System 2018), the policy of designing New-Breed Graduate Programs was launched by the Thai Government in January 2018 and requested to be applied by August 2018 with the aim to serve The Twelfth National Economic and Social Development Plan (2017–2021) (Office of the Prime Minister, Office of the National Economic and Social Development Board 2017) and to promote economic growth in 10 targeted areas (Bunsupaporn 2017): First S-Curve or older industries (Next-Generation Automotive; Smart Electronics; Affluent, Medical and Wellness Tourism; Agriculture and Biotechnology; and Food for the future) and New S-Curve or future industries (Robotics; Aviation and Logistics; Biofuels and Biochemicals; Digital; and Medical Hubs).

To serve such a policy, New-Breed graduates to be developed within this framework are divided into three groups:

1. Vocational certificate and high-vocational certificate students who wish to continue their studies up to HE;
2. Year-3 and Year-4 undergraduates who can shift from their current program to the New-Breed one; and
3. Graduates and workers who want to acquire higher professional skills and matriculate within non-degree programs within 3–6 months.

These 'urgent' New-Breed Graduate Programs have directly affected HEIs throughout Thailand as the framework was open to all universities to submit an unlimited number of programs by February 2018. Nonetheless, only Thai HEIs designing the programs in accordance with the criteria determined by the Office of the Higher Education Commission (e.g., readiness of fundamental facilities, capacity to produce graduates who can fulfill the programs' demands and serve those targeted 10 industries, apprenticeship in real enterprises not less than 50% of the whole learning duration) are to be selected. This current situation in Thai HEIs reflects 'a global effect to a butterfly' instead of a butterfly effect to the globe. That is, according to the Thai Organic Trade Association (2011), 'Thailand is predominantly an agriculture-based country.' Transforming it into an industry-based country at once probably takes years or decades, especially when the concept needs to be combined with the whole country's HE curriculum. Those involved such as administrators, teachers, students, operational staff, parents, and stakeholders need to see the same goal and work together in order to make each curriculum efficient. For instance, if the New-Breed Graduate curriculum does not serve the needs of parents or students, individuals will not be motivated to enroll in it. Likewise, if the curriculum does not meet the requirements of stakeholders, what students have learned will be simply a waste of time. This does not count the time consumed by administrators, lecturers, and operational staff spent writing the curriculum. Nevertheless, as the Thailand 4.0 policy influenced by globalization has been launched, Thai HEs cannot avoid following it. The strong and gigantic wave of globalization has already hit the HE shore within Thailand. The resulting questions are: How destructive is the attack? What is damaged? Are there to be any survivors at all?

5-HE Shields to Safeguard Global Waves: A Case Study of Naresuan University

Ready or not, as of this writing Naresuan University has committed to the national policies, Thailand 4.0 and New-Breed Programs, and already submitted 11 programs to the Office of the Higher Education Commission (Naresuan University, Division of Academic Affairs 2018b). Even though the programs were not chosen, the university's achievement lies on the job which all staff did together, not the acceptance of those programs. To provide a context for this overall endeavor, it is important to note that Naresuan University was developed from a College of Education in 1967, established as the Phitsanulok Campus of Srinakharinwirot University in 1974, and granted official university status and graciously given the name by His Majesty, the latest King Bhumibol Adulyadej, in 1990 (Naresuan University 2014). Compared to the eight Thai universities ranked within the world rankings, Naresuan University is a smaller and newer HEI which will have its 30th Anniversary in 2020. Currently, the university is included within the 300–350 range in the QS Asian University Rankings 2017–2018 and mentioned as an institution which produces students who 'not only need to be well-equipped with academic knowledge but also current issues and global trends in order to cope well with the challenges of the ASEAN Economic Community and be outstandingly qualified graduates who are in demand in the labor market' (Quacquarelli Symonds 2018b).

Given the university's provincial characteristics and qualifications, it is accepted that the global wave that has impacted Naresuan University has been quite harsh. The impacts (perceived by many as 'damage') are rather high because faculties and colleges were asked to design New-Breed programs within a very short period of time and with limited preparation. Yet, the university has survived and moves on; the new programs have been submitted, even as older programs still in the development stage have been requested to follow the New-Breed Graduate criteria (Naresuan University, Division of Academic Affairs 2018a). The important point is not the success developing such program submissions in time, but, rather, following the pathway of the so-called 5-HE Shields which are designed to sustain and protect the essence of Naresuan University from the possible negative effects of seeking to transition to meet the demands of global standards and relevance too quickly.

1st HE Shield: Curriculum Reform

At Naresuan University, the curriculum of the three clusters that constitute the core of the academic program (the Health Sciences Cluster, the Science and Technology Cluster, and the Social Sciences Cluster) is usually revised and updated on a five-year schedule. However, with the adoption of the Thailand 4.0 policy and New-Breed Graduate Programs, each curriculum is now required to be more international, cultural, and practical in preparing students for their future lives. Some clusters or components of clusters may be 'closed' whereas others will be 'opened,' depending on the perceived global needs and estimations of students' future careers. Nevertheless, it is necessary to consider students within a local context (e.g., learning ability, language performance, financial support, learner's needs) as well as in the context of global demands and creating university income. The university has also been cooperating with Thai massive open online course (MOOC) and encouraging teaching staff to produce MOOC programs to meet students' lifelong learning needs (Naresuan University 2018).

2nd HE Shield: Student/Staff Exchange

The university has offered student/staff exchanges (inbound/ outbound) to establish 'international' and 'national' awareness. At present, there are 53 foreign undergraduates (from Bhutan, Cambodia, China, Gambia, Japan, Lao People's Democratic Republic, Malaysia, Myanmar, Pakistan, and Philippines); 157 foreign postgraduates (from e.g., England, Jordan, Indonesia, and African countries); plus 122 full-time foreign teachers (e.g., British, American, Filipino, Japanese, Chinese, French) (Naresuan University, Division of International Development 2018a). Many Thai students have been sponsored to study aboard, either in summer or degree courses, via MOUs and MOAs with 153 foreign HEIs (Naresuan University, Division of International Development 2018b). Even though the number of exchanges is not significantly high, at least it indicates a good start to follow what is a rapid global trend even if at the moment it is progressing at relatively slow speed.

3rd HE Shield: Training Courses

Realizing students' and staff's limited abilities in English and other foreign languages, the university encourages them to be trained at the NU Language Center, within Thailand and abroad. The university also offers courses in Thai languages and activities related to Thai culture, offered to both foreign students and university staff. The aim is to break language barriers which might prevent students and staff from studying and communicating internationally. At this point, the results may not be extremely impressive as the English proficiency of many students and staff is between A1 and A2 levels. The university, however, continues to support developing their proficiency and trying to support them in multiple ways, such as providing English Proficiency Enhancement (EPE) Courses for postgraduate students to help them reach the Common European Framework of Reference for Languages (CEFR) Level with the Cambridge English Placement Test (CEPT) Standard (Naresuan University, Graduate School 2017).

4th HE Shield: Classroom Performance

Many course syllabi at Naresuan University allow students to be exposed to 'foreign' languages and cultures, seeking to provide them with 'international' and 'national' insights through subjects studied. For example, in the British and American Drama course, year-3 students were assigned to read the first act of Peter Shaffer's *The Royal Hunt of the Sun* and perform it as a play one week later (Patamadilok 2017). The result turned out positive and with some guidelines from the lecturer, students could interpret the literary text, including that of Red Indians' culture and history, through what emerged as an excellent performance, with creative costumes and props. They were also asked to perform the British play *The Importance of Being Earnest* by Oscar Wilde as their class thesis and present it as a professional drama production. The outcome was significantly positive, and their performance was appreciated by university administrators, lecturers, and students in the audience (Naresuan University 2017).

5th HE Shield: Research Projects

The university encourages staff and students to engage in research projects. For example, the year-4 students at the Faculty of Education are required to write a 'baby thesis' or conduct a basic research study with their supervisors (Naresuan University, Faculty of Education 2018). Postgraduate students in all faculties are required to write their theses in English and get them published through the TCI/SCOPUS standard. Teaching staff are funded to do a research project every year and have their work published in both national/international journals.

The 5-HE shields are probably common in other Thai universities or HEIs elsewhere. As Sinhaneti (2011) has indicated, Shinawatra University copes with global challenges through multiple collaborations such as acquiring international cooperation, offering international programs, being a venue for educational fairs, increasing regional and international recruitment, spinning out new types of relevant businesses, and focusing on community-driven and societal development. However, the details of 5-HE Shields are probably worthwhile to look at as they not only prevent the hazardous clash of nationalism and internationalism, but also promote understanding and harmony for the two polarities through learning, working and doing activities among Thai, foreign students and staff.

The basis of dealing with these global waves through the shields is their focus on promoting empathy, understanding and cross-cultural awareness. They are also operated with a '3PBL framework,' a problem-based learning approach that focuses on a question-answer approach by teachers (e.g., modest research studies); project-based learning, which emphasizes skill practices after content achievement of students at all levels (e.g., drama performance); and profession-based learning concentrated on developing apprenticeships among students to prepare them for employment or further work after graduation.

These 3PBL operations can be supported by open online course programs that promote knowledge, skills and technology transfer. In terms of knowledge, the programs are required to serve global needs and markets, seeking to support the development of innovative university products such as good textbooks/books (written by lecturers or with international publishers), teaching equipment (IT devices, computer programs), curriculum (modernized), course syllabi (updated), and research studies (joint projects). In their realization, such products should be international. Regarding skill development within the curriculum, it is necessary that

Table 10.1 5-HE Shields' approaches (Table created by author)

5-HE	Shields
1. Curriculum reform	– Cooperation from all parties involved (faculties, divisions, and departments) – Administrators' agreement (top-down policy) – Staff's acknowledgement and realization and action towards policy/university goal
2. Student/Staff exchange	– Regular and Accessible announcement of scholarships – Preparation for applicants and those who obtain scholarships: body of knowledge, language training, cultural awareness, orientation, etc.
3. Training course	– For staff and students: development of language skills (especially English), personality development, leadership, teaching methodology, etc.
4. Classroom performance	– Emphasis on English communication in all subjects – Students' presentations (i.e., TED Talks are applied in many faculties: ED-TALK in the Faculty of Education), competitions, etc.
5. Research project	– Support for research projects in all areas in terms of funding, encouragement, publication, position progress, etc.

lecturers produce or generate practicum curricula to encourage learners to read/study through media in English (or other languages), especially via the Internet. Consequently, such media should be highly communicative. Finally, technology should be employed to create short courses for a workforce/aging society through MOOCs. This has been currently envisaged, transformed, and changed in accordance with university policy.

According to the description, 5-HE Shields' approaches at Naresuan University can be summarized as in Table 10.1.

Epilogue

From a bird's eye view, the idea probably seems too much of an 'ideal' or nearly 'impossible' occurrence because of the amount of effort and collaboration required from all parties involved from the top to the bottom of the academic structure. From a Thai provincial university's perspective, nevertheless, the idea is 'challenging' and 'moving' within the context of a developing HEI because there is no defined pressure from any world-class requirements or expectations. Although the challenges of global trends come to the institution 'at high speeds' and their impact can be damaging, HE within such a provincial setting can survive through the emphasis on promoting mutual understanding and fostering support toward each other within institutional settings. Naresuan University has proved that taking slow steps together can help the institution transition through the global-butterfly effect. At the stage where people are required not only to cope with an 'internationalism' to which they do not belong, but also retain a sense of 'nationalism' which tends to fade way under such circumstances, it is hoped that developing norms of 'harmonious' HE will be a device which helps human beings learn to remain themselves and live with others in this wildly changing world.

REFERENCES

Abdulsattar, T. 2013. Does Globalization Diminish the Importance of Nationalism? *E-International Relations*, November 14. University of New South Wales. Retrieved March 20, 2018 from http://www.e-ir.info/2013/11/14/does-globalization-diminish-the-importance-of-nationalism/.

Alvesson, M., and M. Benner. 2016. Higher Education in the Knowledge Society: Miracle or Mirage. In *Multilevel Governance in Universities: Strategy, Structure and Control*, ed. J. Frost, F. Hattke, and M. Reihlen, 75–90. Basel, Switzerland: Springer.

Balabanis, George, Adamantios Diamantopoulos, Rene Mueller, and T.C. Melewar. 2001. The Impact of Nationalism, Patriotism and Internationalism on Consumer Ethnocentric Tendencies. *Journal of International Business Studies* 32: 157–175. Retrieved March 20, 2018 from https://doi.org/10.1057/palgrave. jibs.8490943.

Boonpen, W. 2015. Jak lok su Thai tid tang mai kong kan reanroo su satawat ti yee sib-ed [From the World to Thailand, a New Direction of 21st-Century Learning, Change the Class, Change the Future]. In Pakee pattana taksa satawat ti yee sib-ed [Development Association for 21st-Century Skills]. *Creative Thailand*, March 29, 2015 and April 1, 2014. Retrieved March 18, 2018 from http://www.tcdc.or.th/creativethailand/article/TheSubject/25279.

Broad, M. 2016. Why Is Globalization Under Attack? *BBC News*, October 6. Retrieved October 12, 2017 from http://www.bbc.com/news/business-37554634.

Bunsupaporn, K. 2017. New Wave of Business Opportunities in the EEC. Siam Commercial Bank, Economic Excellence Centre, June 14. Retrieved March 22, 2018 from https://www.scbeic.com/en/detail/product/3629.

Chalapati, S. 2007. The Internationalisation of Higher Education in Thailand: Case Studies of Two English-Medium Business. PhD thesis, RMIT University, School of Global Studies, Social Science and Planning (Design and Social Context Portfolio).

Collins, M. 2015. The Pros and Cons of Globalization. *FORBES: Reinventing America*, May 6. Retrieved October 12, 2017 from https://www.forbes.com/sites/mikecollins/2015/05/06/the-pros-and-cons-of-globalization/#6e26fa8bccce.

Delanty, G. 2004. Does the University Have a Future? In *Globalization & Higher Education*, 241–254. Honolulu, HI, USA: Hawaii University Press.

Edutopia. 2012. Singapore's 21st-Century Teaching Strategies, March 14. Retrieved March 15, 2018 from https://www.youtube.com/watch?v=M_pIK7ghGw4.

Fairbrother, G. 2003. The Effects of Political Education and Critical Thinking on Hong Kong and Mainland Chinese University Students' National Attitudes. *British Journal of Sociology of Education* 24 (5): 605–620. https://doi.org/10.1080/0142569032000127161.

Grapragasem, S., A. Krishnan, and A.N. Mansor. 2014. Current Trends in Malaysian Higher Education and the Effect on Education Policy and Practice: An Overview. *International Journal of Higher Education* 3 (1): 85–93.

Hazelkorn, E. 2015. *Rankings and the Reshaping of Higher Education: The Battle for World-Class Excellence*. London: Palgrave Macmillan.

Hendrix, M. 2012. The New Era of Globalization. In 2018 The U.S. Chamber of Commerce Foundation. Retrieved March 17, 2018 https://www.uschamberfoundation.org/blog/post/new-era-globalization/33906.

Kong, L.S. 2014. Preparing Graduates for the Workplace of the 21st Century. ASAIHL Conference 'Education Innovation for Knowledge-Based Economy: Curriculum, Pedagogy & Technology,' December 3–5, Nanyang Technology University, Singapore. Retrieved March 10, 2018 from http://conference.ntu.edu.sg/asaihl/Documents/PPTs/1_1%20Prof%20Lee%20Sing%20Kong.pdf.

Kubota, R. 2002. The Impact of Globalization on Language Teaching in Japan. In *Globalization and Language Teaching*, ed. D. Block and D. Cameron, 13–28. London: Routledge.

Lauhathiansind E., and N. Chunbundit. 2016. Thai Higher Education. In *The Palgrave Handbook of Asia Pacific Higher Education*, ed. C. Collins, M. Lee, J. Hawkins, and D. Neubauer. New York: Palgrave Macmillan.

Lavankura, P. 2013. Internationalising Higher Education in Thailand: Government and University Responses. *Journal of Studies in International Education* 17 (5): 663–676, March 19. Retrieved March 19, 2018 from https://doi.org/10.1177/1028315313478193.

Lincicome, M. 1993. Nationalism, Internationalisation, and the Dilemma of Educational Reform in Japan. *Comparative Education Review* 37 (2) (May): 123–151. Retrieved March 20, 2018 from https://doi.org/10.1086/447179.

Ministry of Education, National Education Information System. 2018. New-Breed Graduates, January 30. Retrieved March 24, 2018 from http://www.moe.go.th/moe/th/news/detail.php?NewsID=50575&Key=news_Teerakiat.

Naresuan University. 2014. NU History. Retrieved October 11, 2018 from http://old.nu.ac.th/en/a1_history.php.

Naresuan University. 2017. ED Students Perform Classic and Joyous Play "The Importance of Being Earnest" Following Career Path of Qualified English Teachers, December 7. Retrieved January 5, 2018 from http://old.nu.ac.th/en/gallery1_view.php?n_id=479&img=1&action=view.

Naresuan University. 2018. Invitation to NU Lecturers to Submit Programs and Get Support in Developing MOOC Programs for Thai Cyber Universities' Open-System Instruction Project: Phase 2. Retrieved March 27, 2018 from https://www.nu.ac.th/?p=7693.

Naresuan University, Division of Academic Affairs. 2018a. A Development of New-Breed Graduate Programs for Lifelong Learning (by Associate Professor Dr. Rosarin Wongwirairat). A Workshop on a Design of New-Breed Graduate Programs, March 26, QS 4401, Naresuan University.

Naresuan University, Division of Academic Affairs. 2018b. Memorandum on Submission of New-Breed Graduate Programs (ref. 0527/04061), March 22. Division of Academic Affairs, Office of the President, Naresuan University.

Naresuan University, Division of International Development. 2018a. The Updated List of Foreign Students in 2017. Division of International Development Database, Naresuan University.

Naresuan University, Division of International Development. 2018b. The Updated MOUs and MOAs in 2017. Division of International Development Database, Naresuan University.

Naresuan University, Faculty of Education. 2018. Bachelor of Education Programs. Retrieved October 15, 2017 from http://www.edu.nu.ac.th/th/course/index.php.

Naresuan University, Graduate School. 2017. Announcement of Naresuan University on EPE (English Proficiency Enhancement) to Move up Graduate Students' English Proficiency.

National Science and Technology Capability. 2017. Retrieved March 24, 2018 from https://www.nstda.or.th/th/nstda-doc-archives/thailand-40/11625-blueprint-thailand-4.

OECD. 2009. Globalization and Higher Education: What Might the Future Bring? IMHE-Info, December. Retrieved March 21, 2018 from http://www.oecd.org/education/imhe/44302672.pdf.

Office of the Prime Minister, Office of the National Economic and Social Development Board. 2017. The Twelfth National Economic and Social Development Plan (2017–2021). Retrieved March 24, 2018 from http://www.nesdb.go.th/nesdb_en/ewt_w3c/main.php?filename=develop_issue.

O'Neil, J. 2017. Globalization Has Made the world a Better Place. *The* Guardian, January 18. Retrieved October 12 from https://www.theguardian.com/business/2017/jan/18/globalization-world-trade-asia-global-poverty.

O'Rourke, K.H., and Jeffrey G. Williamson. 2002. When Did Globalization Begin? *European Review of Economic History* 6 (1) (April 1): 23–50. Retrieved March 18, 2018 from https://doi.org/10.1017/S1361491602000023.

Partnership for 21st Century Learning. 2007. Framework for 21st Century Learning. Retrieved February 15, 2018 from http://www.p21.org/our-work/p21-framework.

Patamadilok, S. 2017. Introduction to British and American Drama (205345): A Compiled Textbook. Faculty of Education, Naresuan University.

Pieterse, J.N. 2012. Twenty-First Century Globalization: A New Development Era. Article (PDF Available) in *Forum for Development Studies* 39 (3) (November): 367–385.

Pologeorgis, N. 2017. How Globalization Affects Developed Countries. *Investopedia*, March 6. Retrieved March 10, 2018 from https://www.investopedia.com/articles/economics/10/globalization-developed-countries.asp#ixzz5AzkXWtoM.

Quacquarelli Symonds. 2018a. QS World University Rankings: Nanyang Technological University. Retrieved March 1, 2018 from https://www.topuniversities.com/universities/nanyang-technological-university-singapore-ntu.

Quacquarelli Symonds. 2018b. QS World University Rankings: Naresuan University. Retrieved March 1, 2018 from https://www.topuniversities.com/universities/naresuan-university.

Quacquarelli Symonds. 2018c. QS World University Rankings: 100 Top Universities. Retrieved March 1, 2018 from https://www.topuniversities.com/university-rankings/world-university-rankings/2018.

Quacquarelli Symonds. 2018d. QS World University Rankings: Thailand. Retrieved March 1, 2018 from https://www.topuniversities.com/university-rankings/world-university-rankings/2018.

Royal Thai Embassy. 2018. Thailand 4.0. Washington, DC. Retrieved March 2018 from http://thaiembdc.org/thailand-4-0-2/.

Scott, P. 2000. Globalization and Higher Education: Challenges for the 21st Century. *Journal of Studies in International Education* 4 (1) (March 1): 3–10.

Secretariat of the House of Representatives, E-Library. 2017. *Academic Focus: Thailand 4.0.* Retrieved March 22, 2018 from https://waa.inter.nstda.or.th/stks/pub/2017/20171114-parliament-library.pdf.

Sinhaneti, K. 2011. Emerging Trends of Thai Higher Education and a Case Study of Shinawatra University in Coping with Global Challenges. *US-China Education Review* B3: 370–381.

Thai Association of Governing Boards of Universities and Colleges. 2018. Retrieved March 17, 2018 from https://tagbth.wordpress.com/.

Thai Organic Trade Association. 2011. Overview of Organic Agriculture in Thailand. Retrieved June 1, 2018 from http://www.thaiorganictrade.com/en/article/442.

Wende, van der M., and J. Zhu. 2015. China's Higher Education in Global Perspective: Leader or Follower in the World-Class Movement? *6th International Conference on World-Class Universities* (*WCU-6*), November 1–4, Shanghai, China. Retrieved March 17, 2018 from http://www.shanghairanking.com/wcu/wcu6/7.pdf.

CHAPTER 11

Knowledge Diplomacy and Worldview Diversity Education: Applications for an Internationalized Higher Education Sector

Sachi Edwards and Yuto Kitamura

Introduction

Higher education (HE) is influenced by globalization in various ways, and efforts to internationalize this sector have been the focus of numerous policy initiatives, research studies, curricular and programmatic developments, and philosophical discussions. A particularly marked manifestation of this broad trend—both in practice and in scholarly literature—is the cross-border movement of students. On a worldwide basis, the number of students who study at higher education institutions (HEIs) outside their home countries is currently approaching three million and is projected to

S. Edwards (✉) · Y. Kitamura
Graduate School of Education,
The University of Tokyo, Bunkyo, Tokyo, Japan
e-mail: yuto@p.u-tokyo.ac.jp

© The Author(s) 2019
D. E. Neubauer et al. (eds.), *Contesting Globalization
and Internationalization of Higher Education*,
International and Development Education,
https://doi.org/10.1007/978-3-030-26230-3_11

143

reach as many as eight million by 2025 (Guruz 2011). This chapter presents a new angle of analysis on the phenomenon of rapidly increasing student mobility by applying the lenses of "knowledge diplomacy" (Knight 2015) and "worldview diversity education" (Ilisko 2017; Mayhew et al. 2014). In particular, this chapter will discuss the potential and the responsibility of HE, through internationalization efforts, to promote understanding of differences in worldview and to temper the recent resurgence of nationalism and xenophobia we are witnessing across the globe.

In the discourse around the internationalization of HE, the concepts soft power and global market competitiveness have become predominant reasons for pursuing increased student mobility (Knight 2015), where "soft power" refers to the use of HE to promote a country's agenda internationally "through attraction rather than coercion" (Nye 2004, p. x). However, alternative discourses are now re-emerging that analyze the potential for an internationalized HE sector (in general) and international student mobility (in particular) to serve as a form of knowledge diplomacy and to develop a new generation with broader, more inclusive worldviews (Knight 2015; Yonezawa et al. 2014). In other words, instead of examining the internationalization of HE for its self-serving potential (in terms of gaining global dominance), some scholars are choosing to consider how it can be used as a force for increased global harmony.

Furthermore, a parallel conversation among HE scholars and policy makers around the world discusses the need for education to serve as a tool to "enhance mutual understanding among different cultures and religions" (ASEAN Plus Three 2007, Section D, 5.2). As a response to the increasing displays of violent religious extremism and rising inter-religious tensions worldwide, many government bodies—and, subsequently, university faculty and administrators—have, in recent years, made more overt efforts to incorporate worldview diversity education as an essential component of their educational initiatives (Halsall and Roebben 2006). Within this discourse, exposure to, and education about, religious diversity and cultural diversity (also known, in combination, as worldview diversity) are deemed necessary for students not only to become more effective global citizens, but also more respectful and compassionate people that will help create sustainable peace globally (Ilisko 2017).

In combining these similar, yet to-this-point distinct, bodies of literature, this chapter seeks to accomplish a number of tasks. Specifically, it seeks to: (a) describe the intersections of HE internationalization, cross-border student mobility, knowledge diplomacy, and worldview diversity education; (b) theorize ways forward for HE globally that reflect the potential for knowledge diplomacy and worldview diversity education in an internationalized HE sector; and (c) suggest future areas of research and scholarship that can help to build more synergy between these two associated discourses and establish a stronger understanding of the way HE internationalization can be used as a means for promoting global peace. To be clear, both knowledge diplomacy and worldview diversity education are fairly new concepts within the field of international HE. This chapter, then, is an attempt to contribute to the development of these concepts and their application for the study and practice of higher education.

THE GLOBAL HIGHER EDUCATION MARKET

In this era of globalization, we have seen the emergence of a global HE market, where students are moving at increasing rates across boarders in the pursuit of HE. To compete in this market, many universities are pursing partnerships with institutions in other countries, especially those within their geographic regions (e.g., North America, Europe, and Asia). Partnerships at the national level, both globally and regionally, are also increasing, as countries seek to facilitate the cross-border movement of students and researchers. An example of this can be found in Europe with the Bologna Declaration of 1999—a joint declaration signed by the 29 European ministers in charge of HE—which launched a series of reforms (called the Bologna Process) aimed at the harmonization of HE in Europe. In concrete terms, the Bologna Process has so far resulted in the Europe-wide adoption of a credit conversion system, a comparable degree system (a three-cycle structure composed of bachelor's, master's, and doctorate programs), and the Diploma Supplement (a document attached to HE diplomas to increase international transparency), among other ways in which educational structures across the countries involved have been tuned into each other (Yonezawa et al. 2014). Furthermore, a European framework of qualification has been developed to explicitly indicate the levels of knowledge, skills, and competences expected to acquire specific qualifications. As a result of the Bologna Process, Europe now has an official European Higher Education Area,[1] consisting of 48 countries, all of which are continuously and collaboratively working toward making their HE systems more compatible for the sake of easier student and researcher mobility.

While Europe is typically seen as the pioneering region with regard to this type of initiative, other regions of the world are also pursuing international collaboration with similar goals in mind. The Association for Southeast Asian Nations (ASEAN), together with China, Korea, and Japan (collectively known as ASEAN Plus Three), for instance, has seen growing inter-university alliances and the development of an official inter-governmental body to support students wishing to study abroad within the region. In addition to exchange programs based on academic exchange agreements between individual universities, the ministers of education in ASEAN Plus Three formally established a working group in 2012 to formulate guidelines for the promotion of quality-assured student exchange within the region.[2] Since 2000, the number of students studying abroad within ASEAN Plus Three has been rapidly increasing, whereas the number of students from these countries studying in English-speaking countries (which was previously the preference) has leveled off (Kitamura 2014). The working group, then, helps to accommodate this trend and also to facilitate continued acceleration in this direction.

Other manifestations of the global HE market include the emergence of international branch campuses, designed to give students an international experience without having to leave their home country, or without having to travel as far. Examples include the Malaysia campus of Australia's Monash University, the Rwanda campus of the USA's Carnegie Mellon University, and the United Arab Emirates campus of the UK's University of Exeter. Even further, some institutions are teaming up to start joint degree programs—such as the joint master's degree in transcultural counseling offered by the University of Maryland (USA) and the University of Malta—or open joint campuses—such as Yale-NUS College, a liberal arts college in Singapore resulting from a collaboration between Yale University (USA) and the National University of Singapore (NUS). Such initiatives have rendered the opportunity to, and options for, study abroad more accessible to those students who may hesitate to leave their countries or regions to study for financial or sociocultural reasons.

These initiatives, while cooperative and collaborative in some respects, are also keenly competitive in that they seek to provide a highly desired good (an international HE experience) in a way that is most attractive and easily accessible to potential students. Furthermore, as funding structures and programmatic demands in HE shift—such as the cases of the USA, UK, and Australia (among others) where administrators and staff are asked to do more with less—many institutions are increasing their efforts to recruit international students as a means of competing for the income generated by tuition and fees (Guruz 2011). Indeed, globalization has, in many ways, come hand-in-hand with a rise in the influence of market forces on the direction of the agenda in the HE sector.

Of course, there are numerous manifestations or indicators of internationalization in HE, including internationalizing curriculum or the development of international ranking systems. However, the topic of student mobility dominates the scholarly discourse on HE internationalization and also represents the vast majority of publicly available data meant to demonstrate and measure internationalization in HE (Williams et al. 2017). In other words, student mobility has become a primary issue through which educators, researchers, and policy makers seek to understand and analyze the existence, impact, and potential of an internationalized HE sector. To this point, however, student mobility has largely been thought of in terms of its potential to contribute to attaining soft power in the knowledge economy, as the following section describes.

SOFT POWER AND THE KNOWLEDGE ECONOMY

Within the context of globalization (generally) and a global HE market (specifically), many governments are racing against one another to increase their academic activities, research, and development in order to gain supremacy in the creation, acquisition, and transmission of knowledge. In many cases, this is because they understand scientific research and intellectual output as important pillars of their foreign policy. As Nye (2004, 2008, 2011) explains, an essential factor in a country's pursuit of political and economic supremacy is its success in the international competition for knowledge production, a concept he calls soft power. Different from hard power (the use of coercion or payment to obtain a desired outcome), soft power relies on the use of attraction, or "the ability to influence the preferences of others" (Nye 2008, p. 95). Soft power is utilized by exporting cultures, ideas, and values in ways that "make others want what you want" (Nye 2008, p. 94), including influencing what students learn, experience, and are exposed to through various educational spaces and initiatives. In this way, students who leave home to pursue HE are often understood as facilitators of cultural export. Thus, as the number of students who do this accelerates and gains more attention, these individuals play increasingly important roles as cultural diplomats in the race to shape the production of knowledge and values worldwide. Indeed, the concept has been adopted with great enthusiasm in the realm of HE globally, both as a justification for continued internationalization and as an argument for increased government investment in HE (Akyea 2016).

At the individual level, studying abroad is typically marketed to students as an opportunity for them to boost their chances of getting a job, a higher salary, or acceptance to graduate school.[3] Since studying abroad increases intercultural communication skills—a valuable attribute in an increasingly globalized and ever-changing economy—a student's experience studying abroad does have the very real potential to make them more highly competitive in the job market (Williams 2005). Furthermore, as it positions these individuals ahead of their counterparts who do not study abroad, it can even lead to a greater likelihood of them assuming higher-level positions in political, economic, cultural, and other fields in the future. This represents yet another way that students who study abroad are valuable agents of soft power in the knowledge economy. When countries recruit international students to study at their institutions, not only are they gaining the financial resources that come with international tuition and fee rates, they are also given the opportunity to influence the opinions, perspectives, and desires of those students who, upon return to their home country, can further influence others (Nye 2008).

Thus, as students who study abroad—both students who leave a country to study elsewhere and students from around the world who come to study in that country—have the potential to be helpful to a country's international agenda, the actors of HE all over the world are thinking strategically about how their human and intellectual resources can be put to optimal use; in other words, how their participation in the global HE market can most optimally impact their power and position on the world stage (Yonezawa et al. 2014). By facilitating the increase of students who study abroad, and also recruiting larger numbers of international students to study in their countries, governments can strengthen their role in the global market in the pursuit of soft power—and many of them are doing just that. It is precisely this reasoning that has dominated the discourse about the phenomenon of student mobility, one that prioritizes self-serving interests of a government or individual students in the context of a soft power competition in the global knowledge economy (Knight 2014b).

ALTERNATIVES TO THE POWER PARADIGM

Nye (2008) suggests that those who "deny the importance of soft power are like people who do not understand the power of seduction" (p. 96). It is not our intention to refute the importance or reality of soft power in the global HE market, or in international politics generally. Rather, we want to present an alternative means of analyzing the phenomenon of student mobility in an internationalized HE sector in order to expand the conversation about its potential impacts on our students, our societies, and the world as a whole. There are two concepts we think are particularly promising in their ability to frame this discourse in a way that sheds new light on the pursuit of increased student mobility: *knowledge diplomacy* and *worldview diversity education*.

KNOWLEDGE DIPLOMACY

The concept of knowledge diplomacy has been discussed since the 1980s, mainly by specialists in international political science and international relations (such as Ryan 1988). However, most of these discussions have focused primarily on international negotiations and competition related to intellectual property rights (patent rights, copyrights, and trademark rights). It is only recently that knowledge diplomacy has come to be examined in a manner reflecting the broad sense of the word *knowledge*, making the concept one that can be understood as an alternative to the power paradigm.

Knight (2015), explains that "The role of international higher education in international relations has traditionally been seen through the lens of cultural diplomacy" (p. 1), whereby student and faculty exchange led to cross-cultural learning of language, arts, sport, food, and literature, among other things typically understood as "cultural." However, as globalization and market forces pose stronger and stronger influences on the HE sector, and as international HE takes on new dimensions (such as branch and joint campuses, collaborative policy declarations, regional and global expert networks), the discourse around international HE has shifted to a power paradigm. Now, administrators and policy makers are "increasingly concerned with justifying international HE's contribution to the economic development" and future political power of a country (Knight 2015, p. 2)—as described by Nye's (2004, 2008, 2011) soft power framework. Despite this shift in thinking, student mobility remains the primary focus of analysis and investigation when it comes to measuring and understanding international HE. Knight (2014a, b, 2015) argues, as do we, that a broader and less self-serving approach to thinking about international HE is needed, one that can be described by the concept of knowledge diplomacy.

Unlike knowledge diplomacy in the way that Ryan (1988) and other scholars of international political science use the term, and unlike "cultural diplomacy" which is usually understood as encompassing only traditional elements of culture (such as language, music, or architecture), the way we present knowledge diplomacy here describes a holistic sharing of knowledge in all fields, including science, technology, math, public health, and other fields not typically included in the descriptor "culture." It also describes an approach to international education that pursues more than just student mobility initiatives; one that includes collaboration across communities, various cultural/ethnic/tribal identity groups, institutions, and governments (among other stakeholders) to create research centers, global information sharing networks, and other forms of innovative knowledge creation. If we consider the type of problems we face as a global community (rising levels of xenophobic nationalism and violent extremism, various forms of environmental degradation, ongoing slavery and gender-based violence, to name a few), we know that our best chance for solving these problems is to put our heads together; to find mutually beneficial forms of collaboration and innovation, that lead to mutually beneficial outcomes.

Importantly, approaching our thinking about international HE from a knowledge diplomacy framework also necessitates that we recognize, and work to prevent or rectify, power imbalances that exist in the knowledge economy (generally) and international HE partnerships (specifically). To be sure, when HE and knowledge production are seen through the lens of soft power, imbalances in outcomes and benefits (favoring more powerful regions, countries, institutions, and/or people) result. To start from the framework of knowledge diplomacy can help shed light on potential imbalances and prepare us to develop truly collaborative initiatives, policies, and research projects, where benefits and solutions are shared fairly among all participants, especially those most in need.

To offer an example of what this might look like, we would like to describe the Science and Technology Research Partnership for Sustainable Development (SATREPS).[4] Since 2008, SATREPS has been facilitating collaboration between Japanese researchers and researchers from developing countries around the world to address concerns related to environmental sustainability, natural disasters, or public health. Funded by the Japanese government, its aims are to connect Japanese researchers with those working on similar issues around the world, to give both Japanese researchers and those in partner countries experience working with people from a different culture and context, and to provide Japanese researchers with more exposure to how their phenomena of interest manifest on-the-ground elsewhere in the world. To this point, SATREPS has funded over 130 projects in 50 countries including: (1) the development of an improved metal mining system in Serbia that is more friendly to the environment and to the health of the region's residents, (2) marine research in Palau aimed at creating an international standard that guides economic development so as not to damage coral reefs and other island ecosystems, and (3) a community-based initiative in Cameroon that promotes cassava farming as both an economically sustainable livelihood for locals and a more environmentally sustainable alternative to current deforestation practices in the area. We do not mean to suggest that SATREPS is in some way flawless or a gold standard by which to judge all other international collaborations. Indeed, there are at least some self-interests at play here, since Japanese researchers do benefit from these experiences. However, that the funding goes toward projects that create real-life solutions to real-life problems plaguing communities in other countries, and that local researchers necessarily work as equal members of the research team, demonstrates the mutuality of benefits enjoyed by all parties through this program. In that way, SATREPS provides an example of the kind of HE internationalization initiative that embraces a knowledge diplomacy approach: It facilitates collaboration in knowledge development across borders, cultures, and regions; it addresses issues and problems that have global implications; it disseminates research outcomes to communities and people beyond HEIs alone; and it provides opportunities for researchers and students in HE to interact with and learn from people from other backgrounds and worldviews.

Worldview Diversity Education

The term "worldview diversity education" is also somewhat new in the area of international HE, but likewise serves as a promising framework to think differently about the role and potential of a globalized HE sector. Some use the terms interfaith, intercultural, or inter-religious education (Engebretson et al. 2010; Wimberley 2003) to describe this notion, that education needs to be purposeful and proactive about exposing students to different ways of thinking, knowing, and believing in order to create acceptance and harmony across these lines of difference. Others call it peace education to highlight the peace-seeking goal of these educational initiatives (Yablon 2007). Still others choose to use "education for global citizenship" as the label for the type of education that promotes awareness and appreciation of cultural and religious diversity, as a means of preparing students to be thoughtful and effective members of an interconnected global society (Schattle 2008). We prefer "worldview diversity education" since it encompasses all of these ideas: that cultural and religious differences should be shared, discussed, embraced, and valued; that our cultural and religious socialization shapes our worldviews in ways that we may not even realize or understand, but that learning about others can help facilitate critical self-reflection; and that developing an appreciation for worldview diversity can help make us more peace-seeking, culturally sensitive, and globally minded individuals. Moreover, it recognizes that all people can and should learn from purposeful interaction with those from other worldviews, not just those from specific religious backgrounds or those who choose to affiliate themselves with a religious group (in other words, "non-religious" people also benefit from examining the way religious socialization has shaped their and others' worldviews).

To this point, "worldview diversity education" has been primarily used in the context of US HE in discourse around building students' religious literacy as a response to increasing religious diversity and tension throughout the country (Mayhew et al. 2014). However, it has begun to make its way into literature elsewhere in the world as well (Ilisko 2017; Miedema and Bertram-Troost 2015), since it serves as a helpful concept for encouraging increasingly "secular" people and societies to join conversations about the need to proactively teach about cultural and religious diversity. Indeed, the growth in religious diversity and tension the USA is currently experiencing is also a global phenomenon, and many governments and educators are thinking carefully about how to address this in a way that can lead to greater peace and harmony—both in their own societies and around the world. In other words, beyond the desire to gain power in the knowledge economy, there is a growing recognition in the international HE community that combatting religious extremism and xenophobic nationalism worldwide will require intentional efforts to build mutual understanding of different perspectives, cultures, beliefs, traditions, and worldviews. In many cases, this is an explicit desired outcome of a country's or region's pursuit of increased student mobility in HE (ASEAN Plus Three 2007; Wimberley 2003).

One thing that research on worldview diversity education shows, related to HE internationalization, is that increased student mobility alone is not going to help us achieve this goal. Simply placing diverse students in the same space (for instance, a university campus, a classroom, or a dormitory) is not sufficient to achieve intercultural understanding or appreciation, and may even have the opposite effect (Brown 2009; Leask 2009; Yeakley 2011). Reduction of conflict, tension, prejudice, or ignorance between those with different worldviews requires carefully structured and facilitated interaction (Pettigrew 1998; Sorensen et al. 2009). So, adopting a framework of worldview diversity for our HE internationalization efforts necessarily means that we have to be more purposeful and proactive in coordinating opportunities for students who study abroad to engage both with each other (that is, international students from other countries) and local students from their host country. Moreover, these interactions need to include overt conversations about their cultural, religious, and worldview differences. Bringing diverse students together for an event that does not overtly address their differences may lead some students to develop a sense of commonality with others, but, it can also lead to continued ignorance and misunderstanding or, worse, a decreased sense of trust or interest in learning about others—especially for those students from marginalized groups (Edwards 2016). To encourage more positive outcomes and a more genuine understanding of worldview differences, programming and pedagogy need to be more explicit about their intent.

An example of this type of programming can be found at a number of universities in the USA, operating from the critical social justice model of Intergroup Dialogue (Zúñiga et al. 2007). While the model applies primarily to courses and student programs aiming to teach about differences in race and gender, some institutions also use it to facilitate courses about differences in worldview stemming from religious identity, national origin, or immigration status. The University of Michigan, for instance, offers a course specifically designed to bring together students who are US citizens with international students to discuss their unique experiences and worldviews as members of those groups.[5] Their model requires that students are recruited and screened in order to ensure well-balanced diversity among participants. It also requires that, through the course, students examine differences, power dynamics, and marginalized perspectives as they pertain to the topic of the course, as a means of forcing the dialogue beyond a superficial exchange of stories and pleasantries. Several other US institutions offer courses using this model to facilitate structured interaction between students from different national, religious, and cultural backgrounds (the University of Maryland, New York University, and the University of Washington to name a few), and the list is growing as the model gains attention. Indeed, there are still improvements that could be made to the Intergroup

Dialogue model, and sometimes these classes do not always go exactly as planned (Edwards 2016). Nevertheless, research has shown that participation in these courses leads to an increased awareness of other worldviews and ability to see other perspectives, improved intergroup relationships and mutual understanding, and a stronger desire and ability to promote worldview diversity awareness to others in their lives (Gurin-Sands et al. 2012). As such, there are important lessons that the international HE community can learn from this approach in attempting to bridge differences in worldview and build global harmony.

THEORIZING WAYS FORWARD FOR PRACTICE, POLICY, AND RESEARCH IN INTERNATIONAL HIGHER EDUCATION

As frameworks for thinking about the potential and the responsibility of HE in a globalized world, knowledge diplomacy stresses that knowledge production should be collaborative and communally beneficial, and worldview diversity education highlights the need for religious and cultural differences to be overtly addressed in order for authentic intergroup understanding to occur. Both of them also encourage attention to power dynamics that impact personal, institutional, systemic, and international relationships and the programs, policies, or other educational initiatives that result from those relationships. When taken together, we can understand that theorizing ways forward for international HE necessitates recognition that: (1) Many of the most dire problems we face are not constrained by political borders, and thus, solutions to these problems should be sought out through international collaboration; (2) thinking of international HE as a tool for political supremacy within a global knowledge economy restricts our ability to engage in knowledge production or share valuable information with the genuine intention of solving global crises; (3) positive intercultural and inter-religious interactions and communication skills can strengthen our capacity for collaborative knowledge production; (4) understanding and appreciating worldview diversity is difficult to do without explicitly examining religious and cultural differences or intentionally confronting hegemony and marginalization along these lines; and (5) incorporating worldview diversity education in our HE internationalization efforts, while also developing internationalization policies and programs that advance knowledge diplomacy, can help train new generations of government, private sector, and civil society leaders to be more solution-oriented, globally minded, peace-seeking, culturally sensitive, and concerned about the well-being of others.

What might an international HE agenda look like if the frameworks of knowledge diplomacy and worldview diversity education were more widely adopted? What kinds of research do we need to pursue in order to make this vision more possible? Of course, answering these questions requires multiple layers of consideration, ranging from practice to policy to research. To that end, we offer some recommendations for how international HE, as a field, can move forward when it comes to pedagogy and student programming at the classroom and institutional level, policy initiatives at institutional and national levels, and research and scholarly discourse for both educators and policy makers.

Regarding student mobility, and the curricular and programmatic initiatives surrounding international students on college campuses, the knowledge diplomacy and worldview diversity education frameworks highlight the need to put more effort into cultivating the sharing of knowledge and worldviews between diverse students. Beyond facilitating increased numbers of students who leave their home countries for HE, we need to pay more attention to the experiences those students (and their local peers) are having throughout the course of their studies—experiences both in and out of the classroom. More specifically, we need to be more overt about identifying and addressing any negative experiences students are having. For instance, we know that, in many cases, international students find it difficult to build relationships with local students, which can lead them to feel negatively about their HE experience, their host country, and the local people or culture (Brown 2009). We also know that religious and cultural differences can exacerbate feelings of separateness or exclusion international students experience in a new country (Zhang and Brunton 2007). So, when designing curriculum, pedagogy, research opportunities, support programs, meal services, entertainment, and any other student-related initiatives, purposefully incorporating opportunities to critically analyze the diversity of knowledge and worldviews present among the group can help address the "elephant in the room" (so to speak) and make all students feel acknowledged and appreciated. In addition to entire courses dedicated to intergroup dialogue (as described previously), faculty in all subject areas should give students the opportunity to discuss how their unique cultures and perspectives relate to interpretation and experience of the course's content, assignments, and activities. Moreover, all university staff that have contact with students (faculty, advisors, support personnel) should be proactive in recognizing when there are instances of isolation or self-segregation among culturally, nationally, or religiously diverse students, and facilitate means through which those barriers can be overcome.

Of course, the details of these actions will/should vary according to the specific contexts in which they occur. To assist with our learning about what kinds of approaches work (or do not), in what ways, and for what type of students or institutions, we need additional research about strategies that are already in place. Indeed, there is some existing literature reporting on such initiatives (Campbell 2012; Leask 2009), but many more examples are needed, both positive and negative, and in a wider range of contexts, in order to further enrich our discourse about how to best enable knowledge diplomacy and worldview diversity education to occur in HE around the world. Moreover, asking faculty and staff to take this kind of action necessarily means that they should be offered training and guidance in how to do so. Developing this kind of skill in all university personnel can help promote the sharing of knowledge and worldviews in more fields, which is valuable for building the capacity of these students to co-produce knowledge with diverse peers through research and development later on in their studies and careers. Additional research on faculty and staff training strategies is also needed; again, in a broad range of cultural, economic, and institutional contexts.

On a larger scale, when it comes to policies related to institutional partnerships, national initiatives, or regional networks in international HE, the frameworks of knowledge diplomacy and worldview diversity education help us see that political power and revenue income should not be our priority. Instead, we should be thinking about how we can solve the crises we collectively face by creating opportunities to learn from each other and produce new knowledge together. To start, perhaps this means that we need to start relying on different indicators to track our progress and/or success in international HE. Simply tracking the number of students who study abroad, for instance, or an institution's position on international rankings, does not tell us how much we are actually doing to reduce intercultural conflict or increase our knowledge sharing potential. Documenting internationalization of HE in terms of students' increased intercultural competencies or globally minded critical thinking skills are much more appropriate determinants of how internationalized our HE has become. Likewise, keeping track of how often our collaborative research initiatives produce outcomes that all participants feel they have benefited from, or the extent to which international partnerships produce greater understanding of respective parties' cultures and conditions would also give us a better sense of the success of HE internationalization from the knowledge diplomacy and worldview diversity paradigms. Creating, and consistently recording, different indicators of internationalization in HE may eventually help provide the kind of data that many administrators, policy makers, and funders want to see when making decisions about the design and implementation of international programs and partnerships.

Ideally, this kind of data would help us to better understand the ways our systems, partnerships, and policies do or do not contribute to knowledge diplomacy and worldview diversity education. With that information, we may be able to advance national or regional guidelines regarding student and researcher mobility that are more likely to produce individuals with improved intercultural communication skills and greater compassion for others. Or, we could draw on the data to more effectively design joint campuses or degree programs so as to encourage fair and just distribution of opportunities and benefits across all communities involved. Perhaps we would even have stronger arguments for why increased funding or staffing is needed for the various offices and departments responsible for coordinating internationalization efforts. All of these would go a long way to humanize international education; to help us think more about the human potential and effects of our initiatives, rather than simply about money and power.

Indeed, much of these ideas rely heavily on a nation's ability to develop and fund the kind of research and programming needed for a true humanization of international HE. Wealthy and developed countries must ask themselves: Who is responsible for and who benefits from improving HE in this way? Ultimately, since HE is one of the primary means of training a society's future leaders, the benefit has the potential to be shared among the populous, and thus, it seems quite natural that a substantial portion of the financial burden would be expected from the public sector (Maruyama 2007). However, when it comes to poor and developing countries, many of whom may be in the early stages of developing their HE systems, different considerations often need to be made. Of particular interest in this discussion may be the way that aid is provided in the realm of HE in developing countries through international alliances and cooperation. Assistance of this sort (consisting of tax revenues in developed countries) has typically come either in the form of funding for joint research projects/institutes or as funding for various development initiatives (Kaneko et al. 2002). In many cases, the former has actually been extremely problematic, since individuals who are rather well off in their domestic context usually end up reaping the benefits, leaving out the truly socially and economically vulnerable. Development assistance, on the other hand, has historically consisted of outsiders from foreign researchers/universities dictating what and how to develop, without adequate consideration of local knowledge or perspectives. An alternative option, one that aligns with the knowledge diplomacy and worldview diversity frameworks, lies somewhere in the middle: aid in the form of funding for research that specifically targets development projects where local and foreign researchers work together as equal partners. To be sure, this model has begun to make its way into the international HE sector, exemplified by the SATREPS program described previously. It is our hope that this model of intellectual development cooperation becomes more widely utilized, and that research into the advantages and challenges of working with this model is further pursued.

Conclusion

The globalization of HE is a phenomenon that is well underway and unlikely to reverse. As our knowledge-based societies expand beyond their national borders, students travel in search of alternative educational opportunities. In response, universities offer various programs, trying to attract as many students as possible. Governments also devise policy measures that support universities and individual students from the standpoint of building national power or for the purpose of realizing a culturally enriched society. In this process, as symbolized by the concept of knowledge diplomacy, the principle of competition is at work between countries that want to develop or attract quality human resources. At the same time, globalization has catapulted religious and cultural intolerance, xenophobic nationalism, and violent acts of extremism to global scales. This has caused governments to turn to HE for assistance in their efforts to reverse these dangerous trends. In these ways, the international HE sector is implicated in many of the most fundamental changes in the international socio-economic environment.

Phenomena such as the globalization of universities and the gathering of students from various religious and cultural backgrounds present an opportunity to cultivate future actors of knowledge diplomacy and worldview diversity education. However, little demonstrative research has been conducted from these perspectives. It is essential that researchers and practitioners interested in the globalization of HE continue to further examine these trends, and develop our knowledge base around how to pursue programs and policies that align with these frameworks. If international HE can develop students' capacities to value one another's perspectives, it is well positioned to contribute positively to the movements countering a wide range of global crises, not the least of which is the growing misunderstanding and intolerance between people who hold differing worldviews. Conversely, if we continue to understand international HE as simply a tool in the global power game, we are hindering our potential as a human race to create a sustainable future for the next generations.

NOTES

1. https://www.ehea.info/ (retrieved May 15, 2018).
2. http://www.mext.go.jo/b_menu/houdou/25/10/1340245.htm (in Japanese) (retrieved May 15, 2018).
3. https://www.iesabroad.org/study-abroad/benefits (retrieved May 15, 2018).
4. https://www.jst.go.jp/global/english/about.html (retrieved May 15, 2018).
5. https://igr.umich.edu/article/intergroup-dialogues (retrieved May 15, 2018).

REFERENCES

Akyea, K.S. 2016. *Higher Education as a Soft Power Asset: The Case of Ghana in ECOWAS* (Unpublished Masters dissertation). University of London, London, UK.

ASEAN Plus Three. 2007. *Cooperation Work Plan 2007–2017.* Retrieved from http://www.mofa.go.jp/region/asia-paci/asean/conference/asean3/plan0711.pdf. Retrieved May 15, 2018.

Brown, L. 2009. International Education: A Force for Peace and Cross-Cultural Understanding? *Journal of Peace Education* 6 (2): 209–224.

Campbell, N. 2012. Promoting Intercultural Contact on Campus: A Project to Connect and Engage International and Host Students. *Journal of Studies in International Education* 16 (3): 205–227.

Edwards, S. 2016. *Critical Conversations About Religion: Promises and Pitfalls of a Social Justice Approach to Interfaith Dialogue.* Charlotte, NC: Information Age Publishing.

Engebretson, K., M. de Souza, G. Durka, and L. Gearon (Eds.). 2010. *International Handbook of Inter-Religious Education*, Part One. London: Springer.

Gurin-Sands, C., P. Gurin, S. Osuna, and B.R.A. Nagda. 2012. Fostering a Commitment to Social Action: How Talking, Thinking, and Feeling Make a Difference in Intergroup Dialogue. *Equity and Excellence in Education* 45 (1): 60–79.

Guruz, K. 2011. *Higher Education and International Student Mobility in the Global Knowledge Economy*, 2nd ed. Albany: SUNY Press.

Halsall, A., and B. Roebben. 2006. Intercultural and Interfaith Dialogue Through Education. *Religious Education* 101 (4): 443–452.

Ilisko, D. 2017. Worldview Education as a Viable Perspective for Educating Global Citizens. In *Re-Enchanting Education and Spiritual Wellbeing: Fostering Belonging and Meaning-Making for Global Citizens*, ed. M. de Souza and A. Halafoff. New York: Routledge.

Kaneko, I., F. Kimura, and M. Yamagishi. 2002. Kotokyoiku shien no arikata (Approaches to Support Higher Education). *Kaihatsukinyu kenkyujoho* 13: 60–97.

Kitamura, Y. 2014. Ryugakusei o meguru kokusaitekina kyoso to kyochou: Asia no genjyo toshite kangaeru (International Competition and Harmonization Over Foreign Students). *IDE Gendai no kotokyoiku* (IDE Higher Education Today) January-February: 51–57.

Knight, J. 2014a. Higher Education and Diplomacy. CBIE Briefing Note http:// www.cbie-bcei.ca/wp-content/uploads/2014/10/Jane-Knight-Briefing-Oct-2014.pdf. Retrieved December 26, 2014.

Knight, J. 2014b. The Limits of Soft Power in Higher Education. *University World News* No. 305.

Knight, J. 2015. Moving from Soft Power to Knowledge Diplomacy. *International Higher Education* 80: 8–9.

Leask, B. 2009. Using Formal and Informal Curricula to Improve Interactions Between Home and International Students. *Journal of Studies in International Education* 13 (2): 205–221.

Maruyama, F. 2007. Kotokyoiku e no kouzaiseishishutsu (Public Expenditures for Higher Education). *Daigakuzaimukeiei kenkyu* 4: 21–34.

Mayhew, M.J., N.A. Bowman, and A.B. Rockenbach. 2014. Silencing Whom?: Linking Campus Climates for Religious, Spiritual, and Worldview Diversity to Student Worldviews. *The Journal of Higher Education* 85 (2): 219–245.

Miedema, S., and G. Bertram-Troost. 2015. The Challenges of Global Citizenship for Worldview Education: The Perspective of Social Sustainability. *The Journal of the Institute of Sustainable Education* 17 (2): 44–52.

Nye, J. 2004. *Soft Power: The Means to Success in World Politics*. New York: Public Affairs.

Nye, J. 2008. Public Diplomacy and Soft Power. *Annals of the American Academy of Political and Social Science* 616: 94–109.

Nye, J. 2011. *The Future of Power: The Means to Success in World Politics*. New York: Public Affairs.

Pettigrew, T.F. 1998. Intergroup Contact Theory. *Annual Review of Psychology* 49 (1): 65–85.

Ryan, M. 1988. *Knowledge Diplomacy: Global Competition and Politics of Intellectual Property.* Washington, DC: Brookings Institution Press.

Schattle, H. 2008. Education for Global Citizenship: Illustrations of Global Ideological Pluralism and Adaptation. *Journal of Political Ideologies* 13 (1): 73–94.

Sorensen, N., B.R.A. Nagda, P. Gurin, and K.E. Maxwell. 2009. Taking a "Hands on" Approach to Diversity in Higher Education: A Critical-Dialogic Model for Effective Intergroup Interaction. *Analyses of Social Issues and Public Policy* 9 (1): 3–35.

Williams, J.H., W. Brehm, Y. Kitamura, C. Sam, and R. Shibata. 2017. Internationalization of Higher Education in the Asia-Pacific: Toward a Mapping of Indicators and Their Utilization.

Williams, T.R. 2005. Exploring the Impact of Study Abroad on Students' Intercultural Communication Skills: Adaptability and Sensitivity. *Journal of Studies in International Education* 9 (4): 356–371.

Wimberley, J. 2003. Education for Intercultural and Interfaith Dialogue: A New Initiative by the Council of Europe. *Prospects UNESCO* 33 (2): 199–209.

Yablon, Y.B. 2007. Contact Intervention Programs for Peace Education and the Reality of Dynamic Conflicts. *Teachers College Record* 109 (4): 991–1012.

Yeakley, A. 2011. In the Hands of Facilitators: Student Experiences in Dialogue and Implications for Facilitator Training. In *Facilitating Intergroup Dialogues: Bridging Differences, Catalyzing Change,* ed. K.E. Maxwell, B.R.A. Nagda, M.C. Thompson, and P. Gurin, 23–39. Sterling, VA: Stylus Publishing LLC.

Yonezawa, A., Y. Kitamura, A. Meerman, and K. Kuroda. 2014. *Emerging International Dimensions in East Asian Higher Education.* Dordrecht: Springer.

Zhang, Z., and M. Brunton. 2007. Differences in Living and Learning: Chinese International Students in New Zealand. *Journal of Studies in International Education* 11 (2): 124–140.

Zúñiga, X., B.R.A. Nagda, M. Chesler, and A. Cytron-Walker. 2007. Intergroup Dialogue in Higher Education: Meaningful Learning About Social Justice. *ASHE Higher Education Report* 32 (4): 1–128.

CHAPTER 12

Institutional Social Capital and Chinese International Branch Campus: A Case Study from Students' Perspectives

Yuyang Kang

INTRODUCTION

The recent rise in international branch campus (IBCs) has been meteoric. In 2014, more than 5000 Chinese students went to IBCs in China, compared with less than 600 in 2004 (Ministry of Education [MoE] 2015). In 2016, there were six IBCs operating as independent legal entities in China. The growing trend of IBCs has caught scholars' attention. However, most existing studies on IBCs in China are done from the perspective of the university, the government, and other organizations (think tanks, for example), examining the models and strategies of IBCs (Altbach and Knight 2007; Wilkins and Huisman 2012; Verbik 2015). Only a small portion of existing research focuses on students (Mok and Jiang 2017; The Quality Assurance Agency for Higher Education [QAA] 2012). In all these

Y. Kang (✉)
Lingnan University, Tuen Mun, Hong Kong
e-mail: yuyangkang@ln.hk

© The Author(s) 2019
D. E. Neubauer et al. (eds.), *Contesting Globalization and Internationalization of Higher Education*,
International and Development Education,
https://doi.org/10.1007/978-3-030-26230-3_12

cited cases, little if any attention is paid to the role of institutional social capital and how it influences Chinese IBC students' experiences.

In the special context of IBCs in China, which operate somewhat midway between Chinese and Western cultures, this chapter looks specifically at the role of institutional social capital and how it influences Chinese students' university experiences. Empirical data was gathered through in-depth interviews with current students and graduates of one IBC in China (IBC-A, hereafter). This chapter argues that although certain aspects of institutional social capital may be curtailed, students still have many chances to cultivate their social capital in an IBC context. However, the most commonly addressed function of institutional social capital (that is, its role in students' job-hunting) was not observed in this research.

LITERATURE REVIEW

A number of social scientists have offered different definitions of social capital based on their varied research fields (Adler and Kwon 2002; Bourdieu 1986; Fukuyama 1997). A thorough review of this literature is beyond the scope of this chapter. Here, we focus on literature that is particularly relevant to the sociology of education.

Pierre Bourdieu is regarded as the first contemporary sociologist to systematically analyze social capital. He defines the concept as "an aggregate of resources that are linked to possession of a durable network of more or less institutionalized relationships of mutual acquaintance or recognition" (Bourdieu 1986, p. 248). Bourdieu also claims that social capital, together with economic capital and cultural capital, can determine an individual's chance of success (Bourdieu 1986). He points out that social capital is not a natural given and is established through investment in social networks or relationships with the expectation of returns in the future. Group membership that provides tangible rewards is an essential form of social capital; such groups can be school, college, university (among other things), or sub-groups within these institutions. Bourdieu's definition was pioneering as it pointed out the fungibility of social capital and other forms of capital. However, the process of how social capital reduces into other forms of capital was largely unknown and not amenable to quantified measurement (Portes 1998). Coleman (1988) refined Bourdieu's analysis by including a mechanism for how social capital could create human capital and the consequences of this process. He claimed that social capital can play an essential role in an individual's status attainment activities, which includes educational credentials and easier access to possible jobs (Coleman 1988).

Both Bourdieu's and Coleman's theories show that social capital as an essential resource. By adapting Bourdieu's or Coleman's theoretical framework, early research on education and social capital mainly focused on parents as transmitters or actors of social capital (Dika and Singh 2001). Most of the research involves large-scale panel studies using parental education, family structure, parents' expectation of the child, and parent–teen discussions as indicators of social capital (Hofferth et al. 1998; Wright et al. 2001). Thus far, minimal attention has been paid to the correlation between social capital and students' interaction with peers or teachers at school.

Brinton (2000) was the first scholar to introduce the concept of "institutional social capital." It defined the institutional social capital as "the resources inherent in an organization, such as a school, and thereby available to members of that institution" (Brinton 2000, p. 289). Members of a school, university, or college can accumulate social capital either through intense interaction with other members of these institutions or by involving themselves with exclusive social networks, such as alumni networks. While Brinton (2000) discussed the role of institutional social capital in relation to job engagements of Japanese high school graduates, other scholars have also applied the term to research in other contexts (Waters 2007; Hall 2011). However, there is very little in this body of literature mentioning the context of IBCs in students' home countries, and none looking specifically at the social and cultural contexts of Mainland China largely, which differs greatly from other regions.

Relatedly, Walder (1988) developed the concept "organized dependence." He argued that because of historical and cultural circumstances, Chinese citizens, especially those who work for state-owned enterprises (SOEs), are not just economically dependent on the SOEs, but also politically and personally dependent on the communist party and their supervisors (Walder 1988). Aside from good wages, memberships in an SOEs also provide other nonwage benefits, rights, specific distributions, and welfare entitlements bounded with the identity (Walder 1988). Although the planned economic system in China has declined, the institutional culture endures. Therefore, institutional social capital theory has special significance for research on Chinese students, but scant literature on the internationalization of Chinese higher education (HE) has addressed it. By critically reflecting upon existing literature, this research provides empirical evidence on how institutional social capital influences Chinese IBC students' university experiences.

RESEARCH METHOD

Data for this research was collected through both in-depth interviews and surveys. Semi-structured interviews were conducted with 12 current IBC-A students and graduates, and three current and former IBC-A staff members. Participants were recruited through snowball and intercept sampling, and the sample represents a diverse mix of genders, places of residence, and subjects of study. Additionally, 24 surveys were conducted with IBC-A students and graduates using both an online survey tool and paper questionnaires. The survey was designed in English and then translated into Chinese by the author. All participants were well informed about the purpose of the research and their rights. The first part of the survey asked the participant's background information, which includes gender, age group, place of residence, subject studied, and overseas studying experience. The second part contains questions about students' experiences at IBC-A. Students were asked to respond to statements regarding teaching style, portion of foreign faculty, and academic environment, among other topics. Answers were given using a 5-point Likert scale, which ranged from "completely disagree" to "completely agree." Another 24 questions were about students' motivations for choosing IBC-A. Questions were designed based on prior findings about how students evaluate their HE experiences. Questions in this part of the survey used a 5-point Likert scale ranging from "not important at all" to "extremely important." There were 45 questions in total, and the respondents could volunteer to participate further in an in-depth interview by providing their contact information at the end of the questionnaire.

Of the 15 total interviews conducted, most of the interviews took place at IBC-A campus, but some alumni and former staff members were also interviewed through Skype. The interviews took a semi-structured format, and each interview lasted for 20–40 minutes. Most of the interviews were recorded and later transcribed into written notes. For unrecorded interviews, notes were made during the interview itself. Thematic analysis was used to analyze findings from interviews.

IBC-A is a good representation of Chinese IBCs, as it is one of the very first Sino-foreign joint venture universities to receive approval from the Chinese Ministry of Education (MoE). University A from the UK and B

Education Group (B Group, hereafter), which is a Chinese private educational company, jointly developed it. It has been operating for more than ten years and is approaching a stable development stage. Compared to other IBCs in China, it has a much bigger volume of students. Therefore, it is a good case for studying students in Chinese IBCs.

Qualitative research is sometimes criticized for the generalizability of the findings to other settings because sample sizes are usually much smaller than those of quantitative research (Bryman 2016). It is also thought that qualitative research sometimes might be too subjective (Bryman 2016). However, after reviewing the existing literature, the author believes that a qualitative method better fits the purpose of this study and can better contribute to current research in this field. Most existing studies on students' experiences use quantitative methods, such as questionnaires, to construct variables to explain student destination choices. One limitation of these methods is that they are mainly structured by the researchers' presumptions and tend to exhibit more rigidity in the research process, which increases the limitations on participants' responses. In contrast, qualitative research methods, such as in-depth interviews, can provide richer and more detailed information on how and why individuals make particular choices, as well as their lived experiences resulting from those choices.

In addition to data collection methods, it is also worth reflecting upon the type of student choosing to pursue a degree at IBC-A. Current research on Hong Kong students pursuing international degrees at home reveals that these students are less likely to display the traits and privileges that are commonly associated with international study (Waters and Leung 2013). A large portion of those Hong Kong students came from families without a history of getting tertiary education and many worked part-time to fund their studies. In comparison, students who physically went abroad are usually from relatively well-off families and thus can rely on their parents for financial support (Brooks and Waters 2010; Findlay et al. 2012).

In our sample, although the IBC-A students are physically at home like those Hong Kong transnational higher education (TNE) students, they show demographic similarities with students who are actually internationally mobile. A great number of our sample students came from well-educated families where their parents are university graduates. Meanwhile, unlike Hong Kong TNE students, IBC-A students largely rely on families for financial support. In 2012, IBC-A raised its annual tuition fee for undergraduate students from 60,000 Yuan to 80,000 Yuan, which was 15–20 times higher than the fees charged by a typical Chinese public university. According to the Statistical Yearbook of China, the per capita annual income of Chinese urban households was 24,564.7 Yuan in 2012 (National Bureau of Statistics 2015). Therefore, it is reasonable to state only individuals from relatively rich families can afford the tuition at IBC-A. Thus, our sample could suggest that students pursuing international degrees in Mainland China are quite different from Hong Kong students who choose to obtain international qualifications at home. In the following section, I draw upon the empirical data from this study to consider the role of institutional social capital on the experiences of IBC-A students and graduates, focusing in particular on what and how social capital is transmitted and accumulated by students within the IBC.

STUDENTS' SENSE OF SOCIAL NETWORK

This research draws special attention to students' interaction with peers or alumni. In fact, nearly all of the student interviewees (11 out of 12) mentioned they contacted their friends or relatives who were studying at IBC-A before their applications. One of the reasons they offered for doing this is that, as a new phenomenon, IBCs have raised debates not just within the scholarly community but also among students and parents. Whereas education institutions and policy makers arguing about potential intellectual brain drain or whether setting IBCs can be a strategic mistake (Shattock 2007), students and parents are more concerned about teaching quality and campus life.

Altbach (2015) claims that the "product offering" abroad rarely comes close to that at the home campus, in terms of the breadth of curriculum, the quality of academic staff, the physical environment, the learning resources, and the social facilities (Altbach, p. 2). As it is usually difficult to lure home faculty to branch campuses for a long period of time, branch campuses usually hire faculty and staff that lack an affiliation or experience at the home campus (Altbach 2015). Also, it is difficult for branches to replicate the breadth of curriculum or research opportunities, as this requires talented scholars, a free research atmosphere, and great investment in infrastructure and facilities. Contrary to Altbach's criticism (QAA)'s 2012 report states that the academic standards and the quality of student learning experiences at IBC-A are equivalent to those of University A in the UK. In terms of other curriculum, the report phrases "students at the [IBC-A] received as fully a British education as it is possible to provide in China" (QAA 2012, p. 11). Nevertheless, this vague statement by the QAA certainly is not enough to prevent students and families from having questions about enrolling at an IBC.

Beyond the scholarly community, there are debates among Chinese citizens and students on the Internet. While some online comments claim that IBC-A is one of the best universities in China, providing a unique international education to students, others see the university as an average Chinese university with nothing special but high tuition fees.[1] Conflicting views on the Internet may confuse potential students; therefore, they reach out to people in the real world for advice. Interviewee Y, an IBC-A graduate of International Communications, said:

> A relative of mine happened to be studying at IBC-A, so I contacted her. She gave me very positive feedback and that helped me to make up my mind in application... I probably would still apply for it even if I knew no one there, but I would definitely think twice if she had a fairly negative attitude towards the university.

Like Y, many interviewees mentioned their friends or relatives who were studying at IBC-A as their sources of information. As online information tends to be controversial and confusing, information from a relative or friend who studied at the university can be of great help to the students in making decisions. This is in accord with Haug's (2008) study on social networks and migration theory that interaction within social networks makes migration easier by providing necessary information and reducing the risks of moving (Haug 2008).

Several students discussed their interest in networking when applying for and studying at IBC-A. Interviewee W, for instance, a third-year student of International Business Economics, reported that he cared more about network opportunities than academic environments when he was choosing an institution.

> Honestly speaking, as long as I can pass the tests and get my degree on time, I don't care too much about the teaching and learning, as I don't think I can learn how to do business from classes. Experiences and opportunities are more important for an entrepreneur's success than the textbook theories, and to get good opportunities in China, one needs to rely on networks.

Like W, many students majoring in business or arts believe that networking opportunities at IBC-A are better than other institutions in China, with *gaokao* (Chinese National College Entrance Examination) scores and high tuition fee as two compulsory requirements for entry. As we have discussed in the former section, only students from relatively rich families can afford the tuition fee of IBC-A. The university enrolls Chinese Mainland students only through the channel of the MoE, which means *gaokao* is the prerequisite. In 2014, the average *gaokao* score of IBC-A newly enrolled students majoring in science was 650, which was 18 points higher than that of Ningbo University and 49 points lower than the average of Zhejiang University. Ningbo University is neither a 985 nor 211 project university while Zhenjiang University is one of the top 10 higher education institutions in China. Although IBC-A usually avoids being compared with other universities in China's public higher education system, the *gaokao* score indicates it is viewed as a good but not top university by Chinese students and their parents.

Brinton's institutional social capital theory mainly focuses on how institutional social capital helps students to find their first jobs, with no emphasis on its role in driving students to apply for a certain school or university. Walder (1988) states how the planned economic system and SOEs have cultivated Chinese citizens' dependence on their working institutions, since SOE membership means not just higher wages but also nonwage benefits and rights. Although most of the citizens of China are no longer SOE members, this institutional culture is still vivid in Chinese society. This helps us to explain why the Chinese IBC students value social capital, especially institutional social capital. The students' attitude is also in accord with Bourdieu's explanation that social capital is established through investment in social networks or relationships with the expectation of returns in the future (Bourdieu 1986). It is fair to say that opportunity to acquire institutional social capital at IBC-A works as a pull factor to attract some students. In the next section, we will discuss what social capital is transmitted to the students.

Social Capital from Teaching and Learning

In IBCs, there is a geographical separation between the home campus and the branch campus. Waters and Leung (2013) also discussed this separation and its implications on the availability of institutional social capital for Hong Kong TNE students. Their research suggests the general administration of these TNE degree programs is primarily conducted by the local institutions, including control over curriculum and course content (Waters and Leung

2013). This research reveals that the story of Mainland China-based IBC differs from Hong Kong programs in several ways.

Faculty Turnover and Impacts on Student Learning Experience

IBC-A is one of the first Sino-foreign joint venture universities to receive approval from the MoE. As China's legislation does not allow foreign universities to set up independent branch campus in China, IBC-A is actually an independent university, despite its name indicating that it is a branch campus of the UK university, University A. The IBC was jointly developed by the University A, and B Education Group, a Chinese private educational company in Zhejiang province. B Group is responsible for the development of the campus infrastructure and daily administration duties. Quality assurance remains the responsibility of the University A, and the delivery and award of all degrees are subject to the provisions of the University's Senate and relevant UK legislation (Ennew and Yang 2009).

IBC-A has two systems of faculty recruitment. University A directly recruits some of the faculty from the UK and those recruited are usually registered at both University A and IBC-A. The Chinese campus also recruits faculty members on a global scale on its own, but the final list of candidates needs to be approved by the home institution in the UK. Faculty members recruited via the latter channel are only signed as IBC-A faculty instead of University A, but most of them are paid at the corresponding UK payment rate. Some of the international scholars are paid even higher salaries than the rate of the UK institution because they may get an extra bonus for working in China. In the meantime, a small portion of the faculty are paid at a lower rate. This case mainly applies to those faculty members who earned their degrees at Chinese institutions.

Interviewee A, a former University A staff who once was a member of the university's Chinese affair office said,

> Some of the staff receive higher payments than the local staff even when they are doing the exact same thing, and I think the existence of inequality can increase the tension within the faculty and undermine people's willingness to stay.

Both students and staff who were interviewed mentioned that teachers tend to stay only for a few years at IBC-A. Some students complained that this makes it difficult to maintain long-term contacts with their teachers.

There are two main reasons behind it. The first is the geographic location of the campus. IBC-A is located in a coastal city in Zhejiang Province. The city has good living environment and economic development, but it is neither a metropolis like Beijing and Shanghai nor a well-known travel destination. Only a few foreign scholars have heard about the city and once they moved to IBC-A, they find limited people with whom they can communicate. Also, scholars with families may be unable to move to IBC-A or China because of family reasons. "*Once I knew a scholar who was really interested in China and he really wanted to work in China, but his children were too young therefore he had to give up the chance*" said interviewee A.

The second reason is that there are limited promotion opportunities at the branch campus. Although the university is trying to enroll more students, it still hard for IBC-A to make its ends meet. So far, the campus is still running a deficit. IBC-A has a much smaller postgraduate student population, which limits its potential for academic expansion and job creation. In 2014, it had 549 postgraduate students and around 600 faculty members. In some departments and schools, it is common that there are more teachers than postgraduate students. After two or three years at IBC-A, many faculty members find it difficult to be promoted and decide to move to other institutions for the development of their careers. Interviewee S, a senior student of civil engineering, said,

> I don't like it. Last year a well-respected scholar left our faculty, and I was really depressed for that because it made me lose confidence in the department. It does not necessarily mean that the new teachers are not good, but they are less familiar with what we have learnt.

Some other students also have similar complaints. After a faculty member leaves for other institutions, some of the students find it difficult to keep in contact, as the teachers would change their contact information too. It also set obstacles for those who need to find references for their further study, which is very common among IBC-A students.

It is noticeable that although a small student body may result in the frequent turnover of faculty, it can also improve students' learning experience at IBC-A. A smaller group of students also means more average access to campus facilities and residence halls. More interaction with classmates and tutors can also intensify the bonding experience between students and faculty members. Existing literature on education experience has proved that small class size can positively affect both the academic achievements and experiences of students (Hoxby 2000; Ehrenberg et al. 2001).

Student's Perceptions of British Education

The results of this research accord with QAA's 2012 report that students at the IBC-A received as fully a British education as it is possible to provide in China (QAA 2012). The education provision of IBC-A has certain UK characteristics like small class size, fewer lectures, and more independent learning and group discussion. However, in most cases, IBC-A is compared to and competing with Chinese HEIs instead of those in the UK or other parts of the world. IBC-A is trying to provide a British education in China, but due to difficulties in recruiting international faculty and students, it has a high portion of Chinese faculty and nearly all of its full-time undergraduates are Chinese nationals. Moreover, some of the IBC-A students may have limited understanding of the nature of UK-style education at the beginning stage.

Students from the Faculty of Science and Engineering tend to hold a negative attitude toward the reduced number of course hours. Interviewee G, a second-year civil engineering student, said the course time of IBC-A was far from enough compared with its Chinese competitors.

> If I want, I can arrange to finish all my classes within two days each week and there are few assignments for me. Some boys do not go to classes for the whole term, but they can still pass as long as they take one or two weeks preparing themselves before the exams. I have some friends who study the same major at other universities and they have to attend lots of lectures and workshops. If they do not work very hard, they will definitely fail the exam. I feel the faculty should provide more modules about basic engineering knowledge and some theories as these are the foundations.

Many students mentioned that they wanted the lecturers to teach more basic knowledge instead of just inspiring them. Tweed and Lehman (2002) point out that one significant difference between Chinese and Western education is that the Western learning tradition believes everyone's knowledge has its limitations and therefore learners should be responsible for exploring the truths for themselves. By contrast, Chinese learning tradition presumes most of the important knowledge is already known. Hence, students can directly learn from the recognized masters. When the author asked this group of students whether they knew IBC-A uses British teaching style, most of them said yes but they also admitted that their expectations of British education were largely based on their own interpretations. Interviewee M, a fourth-year student of architecture environmental engineering, said,

> When I was in my second year, I also had the concern about course hours, but then I found out that there were only 4 to 5 modules at the UK campus too. There are more seminars and available optional modules in the University A and it is definitely true that the academic environment is better than IBC-A, but in terms of teaching methods, they are the same.

An academic year at IBC-A includes two semesters and the second semester consists of two terms, Term 2 and Term 3. Similar to most UK universities, Term 3 is the examination term. For students at IBC-A, each term lasts for 12 weeks and they need to choose 4 to 6 modules for each term. By comparison, Chinese universities usually have just two terms and each lasts for around 20 weeks. Students usually need to finish 20 hours of course attendance each week. The statistics may vary from one university to another and there are slight differences across majors. But overall, it is clear that IBC-A students need to take fewer courses than their peers in Chinese universities and students at the UK-style university are expected to be more independent in learning.

Fewer course hours allow IBC-A students to actively engage in extra-curricular activities and increase their sense of being members of the "corps." Bourdieu (1996) discusses the importance of real solidarity among group members. He states that social capital of elite education institutions operates and reproduces itself based on solidarity among their members (Bourdieu 1996). In IBC-A, students can join many different clubs, where people with the same hobbies can play together. Some of the interviewees complained about too many non-academic activities on campus, but all these students have joined at least one student organization or club and they agreed that these experiences increased their sense of belonging to the university.

IBC-A students may find it difficult to maintain long-term contact with faculty members who move to other institutions, which curtails institutional social capital. However, fewer course hours together with smaller classes and students' intentions to build networks with each other are three factors that contribute to lasting social connections among IBC-A students and alumni.

The Mismatch with the Local Job Market

Studies of social capital, especially institutional social capital, are unequivocal about how institutional social capital helps students to find their first jobs after graduation (Brinton 2000; Hall 2011; Lee and Brinton 1996). However, in this study, there is no strong evidence indicating a correlation between institutional social capital and IBC-A students' first jobs. The main reason is that most of the graduates go on to postgraduate study outside of China instead of finding a local job. Interviews with IBC-A students reveal that most of them believe there are fundamental differences between IBC-A and other Chinese universities and a mismatch between the demands of the local job market and IBC graduates. Interviewee Z, a graduate of international business economics who was enrolled in a master's degree program in the USA, shared why she chose to pursue a master's degree.

> The first reason is the fierce competition among university graduates. Twenty years ago a bachelor's degree can find you an "iron rice bowl," but now, a master's degree is a must for many high-ranking companies. The second, honestly speaking, our university is not well recognized by many Chinese companies because it has short history and the name sounds very similar to those of some third-tier institutions. The final reason is because the teaching and campus environment are very British, therefore many students found it difficult to adapt to local job markets.

Likewise, many other participants also mentioned they were not willing to find a job directly after their graduation from IBC-A. According to the participants, only a few students planned to go directly to work after their four-years' study, and this group of students mainly intended to take jobs in foreign companies or jobs that their families found for them.

The most commonly addressed function of institutional social capital is its role in students' job-hunting. It is interesting to find that most of the students are satisfied with their learning experience at IBC-A and they have sufficient opportunities to bond with peers, but the job-finding effect of institutional social capital is not obvious among the research participants. The reasons why IBC-A students are more likely to further their studies abroad are still largely unknown. This is an issue that deserves more complex research.

CONCLUSION

This chapter has examined the role of institutional social capital in Chinese IBC students' university experiences. It contributes to the current institutional social capital literature by showing its special role in recruitment of Chinese students. Based upon findings generated from interviews with students, this research finds that the assumption that IBCs can provide better institutional social capital is part of the reason why some Chinese students choose to study at an IBC. Because of historical and cultural circumstances, young Chinese individuals being educated in a Western-style university still attach special importance to being a member of certain institutions. It might be difficult for IBC-A students to maintain long-term contact with faculty members who tend to move to other institutions, which curtails some institutional social capital. However, fewer course hours together with smaller classes and students' higher intention to build networks with each other are three factors that contribute to lasting social connections among IBC-A students and alumni. Despite these positive factors indicating the strong potential for developing institutional social capital, the job-finding effect of institutional social capital was not obvious in this research because a large portion of the graduates did not go to work directly after their graduation.

The author also acknowledges the limitations of this study. This is only a short-term case study on one of the IBCs in China and the sample size is small. While this chapter shows some effects of institutional social capital on IBC students, further explanation on how students cultivate their social capital and how their perceptions change over time can only be made after more complicated large-scale participant observation research.

Acknowledgements This chapter is developed from the author's thesis submitted to King's College London. The author would like to thank participants of the International Symposium cum Senior Seminar: Contesting Globalization and Implications for Asian Pacific Higher Education for their valuable comments and advice.

NOTE

1. http://bbs.tianya.cn/post-university-66610-1.shtml   (in   Chinese). Retrieved on 31 May 2015.

REFERENCES

Adler, P.S., and S.W. Kwon. 2002. Social Capital: Prospects for a New Concept. *Academy of Management Review* 27 (1): 17–40.

Altbach, P.G. 2015. Why Branch Campuses May Be Unsustainable. *International Higher Education* 58: 1–3.

Altbach, P.G., and J. Knight. 2007. The Internationalization of Higher Education: Motivations and Realities. *Journal of Studies in International Education* 11 (3–4): 290–305.

Bourdieu, P. 1986. The Forms of Capital. In *Handbook of Theory of Research for the Sociology of Education*, ed. J.G. Richardson, 241–258. Westport, CT: Greenwood.

Bourdieu, P. 1996. *The State Nobility: Elite Schools in the Field of Power*. Stanford: Stanford University Press.

Brinton, M.C. 2000. Social Capital in the Japanese Youth Labor Market: Labor Market Policy, Schools, and Norms. *Policy Sciences* 33 (3–4): 289–306.

Brooks, R., and J. Waters. 2010. Social Networks and Educational Mobility: The Experiences of UK Students. *Globalisation, Societies and Education* 8 (1): 143–157.

Bryman, A. 2016. *Social Research Methods*. Oxford: Oxford University Press.

Coleman, J.S. 1988. Social Capital in the Creation of Human Capital. *American Journal of Sociology* 94: S95–S120.

Dika, S.L., and K. Singh. 2001. Applications of Social Capital in Educational Literature: A Critical Synthesis. *Review of educational research* 72 (1): 31–60.

Ehrenberg, R.G., D.J. Brewer, A. Gamoran, and J.D. Willms. 2001. Class Size and Student Achievement. *Psychological Science in the Public Interest* 2 (1): 1–30.

Ennew, C.T., and F. Yang. 2009. Foreign Universities in China: A Case Study. *European Journal of Education* 44 (1): 21–36.

Findlay, A.M., R. King, F.M. Smith, A. Geddes, and R. Skeldon. 2012. World Class? An Investigation of Globalisation, Difference and International Student mobility. *Transactions of the Institute of British Geographers* 37 (1): 118–131.

Fukuyama, F. 1997. Social Capital and the Modern Capitalist Economy: Creating a High Trust Workplace. *Stern Business Magazine* 4 (1): 1–16.

Hall, S. 2011. Educational Ties, Social Capital and the Translocal (Re)production of MBA Alumni Networks. *Global Networks* 11 (1): 118–138.

Haug, S. 2008. Migration Networks and Migration Decision-Making. *Journal of Ethnic and Migration Studies* 34 (4): 585–605.

Hofferth, S.L., J. Boisjoly, and G.J. Duncan. 1998. Parents' Extrafamilial Resources and Children's School Attainment. *Sociology of Education* 71 (3): 246–268.

Hoxby, C.M. 2000. The Effects of Class Size on Student Achievement: New Evidence from Population Variation. *The Quarterly Journal of Economics* 115 (4): 1239–1285.

Lee, S., and M.C. Brinton. 1996. Elite Education and Social Capital: The Case of South Korea. *Sociology of Education* 69 (3): 177–192.

Ministry of Education. 2015. List of Cooperations Approved by Ministry of Education. *Chinese Foreign Cooperation in Running Schools Information Platform.* Retrieved from http://www.crs.jsj.edu.cn/index/sort/1006. Last accessed July 2019.

Mok, K.H., and J. Jiang. 2017. Massification of Higher Education: Challenges for Admissions and Graduate Employment in China. In *Managing International Connectivity, Diversity of Learning and Changing Labour Markets*, ed. K.H. Mok, 219–243. Singapore: Springer.

National Bureau of Statistics. 2015. *Statistical Yearbook of China.* Beijing: Zhongguo tongji chubanshe.

Portes, A. 1998. Social Capital: Its Origins and Applications in Modern Sociology. *Annual Review of Sociology* 24 (1): 1–24.

Shattock, M. 2007. Overseas Campuses: The Management Perspective. In *Overseas Campuses: The Management Perspective*, ed. A. Fazackerley and M. Shattock, 19–21. London, Agora: The Forum for Culture and Education.

The Quality Assurance Agency for Higher Education. 2012. *Review of UK Transnational Education in China: The University of Nottingham Ningbo Campus.* Mansfield, UK: The Quality Assurance Agency for Higher Education.

Tweed, R.G., and D.R. Lehman. 2002. Learning Considered Within a Cultural Context: Confucian and Socratic Approaches. *American Psychologist* 57 (2): 89.

Verbik, L. 2015. The International Branch Campus: Models and Trends. *International Higher Education* 46: 14–15.

Walder, A.G. 1988. *Communist Neo-Traditionalism: Work and Authority in Chinese Industry.* Berkeley: University of California Press.

Waters, J.L. 2007. 'Roundabout Routes and Sanctuary Schools': The Role of Situated Educational Practices and Habitus in the Creation of Transnational Professionals. *Global Networks* 7 (4): 477–497.

Waters, J., and M. Leung. 2013. A Colourful University Life? Transnational Higher Education and the Spatial Dimensions of Institutional Social Capital in Hong Kong. *Population, Space and Place* 19 (2): 155–167.

Wilkins, S., and J. Huisman. 2012. The International Branch Campus as Transnational Strategy in Higher Education. *Higher Education* 64 (5): 627–645.

Wright, J.P., F.T. Cullen, and J.T. Miller. 2001. Family Social Capital and Delinquent Involvement. *Journal of Criminal Justice* 29 (1): 1–9.

CHAPTER 13

Conclusion

Sachi Edwards and Deane E. Neubauer

In the months that have transpired since the academic meeting held at Lingnan University in November of 2017 that formed the basis for the chapters of this volume, the related phenomena of resurgent nationalism and globalization have continued to engage in various ways throughout the globe. The chapters of this volume serve to illuminate individual aspects of this engagement in a variety of ways. Reviewing them after the fact, as it were, we are impressed by how much our contributors chose to bring forth exemplifications of the tensions between the unstoppable forces of globalization and the nationalist responses to them. The examples discussed in

S. Edwards (✉)
Graduate School of Education,
The University of Tokyo, Bunkyo, Tokyo, Japan

D. E. Neubauer
Asia Pacific Higher Education Research Partnership, East–West Center, Honolulu, HI, USA
e-mail: deanen@hawaii.edu

University of Hawaii at Manoa, Honolulu, HI, USA

© The Author(s) 2019
D. E. Neubauer et al. (eds.), *Contesting Globalization and Internationalization of Higher Education*,
International and Development Education,
https://doi.org/10.1007/978-3-030-26230-3_13

this volume do not necessarily emphasize the intersection of global migration and national policy as it is effectuated within the higher education sphere—although that is, indeed, the backdrop upon which their discussions take place. Instead, the authors featured here chose to focus on efforts by national governments within the Asia Pacific region to advance policies that would likely continue existing policy directions (adapting to globalization changes) in the face of such nationalist energies within the overall international HE sphere.

At the time of this event, the relative importance of nationalist engagements within Asian regional HE was less focused and developed as they were within Western Europe and the United States. In the intervening months between the Lingnan meeting and the final publication of this volume, various elements of the endemic tension between continued globalization and resurgent nationalism have developed further clarity. At the pinnacle is continued global competition that intersects globalization and nationalism, such as the trade and other economic engagements between China and the United States. During this intervening period of roughly 18 months, we have witnessed various formalizations of trade tensions between these two massive economic systems at the heart of the global economy and it is clear that this dynamic will continue to frame the coming decade of global engagements. As we write this concluding chapter, China is reporting the lowest level of economic growth in a decade and the US stock market is fluctuating in response to complex interest rate rumors and negative early income reports from giant American firms (such as Apple) with enormous investments in China (Tan 2019; Phillips 2019). Additionally, in our current global environment, Britain continues its political dance toward Brexit, various internal nationalist engagements continue within Europe (e.g., Germany, France, Italy, Spain, and Sweden), political tensions between the United States and Russia continue to expand, a new nationalist government has taken power in Brazil, Venezuela appears engaged in a regime contest that could result in civil war, and so on. From the standpoint of this volume, we see that the overall context that has come to frame and color higher education continues to be dynamic and subject to change—in some cases, that change may indeed be quite radical.

The ambivalence that is implicit in the foregoing is itself readily apparent in some of the major political economic events of the day. Again, during the process of completing this portion of the book, the World Economic Forum conducted its 2019 annual session in Davos, Switzerland absent the participation of the American President whose own particular nationalist-focused concerns had resulted in the longest shutdown of the US government in history. The topic chosen for the five-day session in Davos was: "Globalization 4.0: Shaping a Global Architecture in the Age of the Fourth Industrial Revolution" (Hohmann and Greve 2019). As Hohmann and Greve's (2019) *Washington Post* article reported, despite the fact that this event is typically attended by the vast majority of world leaders, this year's absences included multiple key global leaders such as Donald Trump (United States), Theresa May (United Kingdom), and Emmanuel Macron (France), who each have ongoing political crises in their own countries. Many observers attributed their absence to the intensity and timing of their respective "nationalist" events—which, in turn, are viewed as repercussions from the globalist pretentions and past policies of their nations— sufficient enough to warrant that particular country's leader not attending the conference. It is certainly reasonable in such contexts (and more that could be adduced) to conclude that an important shift in the nature and pattern of globalization is underway and will certainly be consequential.

The caveat we wish to provide and to imply is represented in various ways throughout the selections in this volume. That is, we want to underscore that in a significant number of ways, nationalism and globalization are large, complex social phenomena that proceed in the world across multiple fronts and directions, and within which nations participate differentially as dictated by their own historical experiences. Even while we can recognize that within common discourse nationalism and globalization can be and are frequently framed and discussed as if they were polar opposites and as if one were necessarily situated in one nation-state or another other, this framing does not in fact describe the complex ways in which the world actually works. More properly, it seems to us, these two massive ways of valuing, organizing, and rationalizing the world—nationalism and globalization— are complex states of being that stand in constant tension with each other. What does seem clear, and that which is clearly represented in the Davos instance and in the kinds of behaviors emanating from a number of countries, is that the balance of tension between these two massive global forces has shifted and may continue to shift away from a ready acceptance of globalization and toward that of various increasing nationalist expressions.

It is also clear that such a movement toward increased tension between these two macro tendencies will come to affect HE across the world in a variety of complex ways. Some of the authors featured in this volume aptly note the tensions various countries are experiencing as they develop their HE systems around the international exchange of students. A country such as Japan, to take a case in point, has during the twenty-first century developed successive programs by MEXT to attract international students, motivated in large part by the need to develop human capital that can effectively lead a globalized society and by the desire to compete for top positions in global rankings. Similar programs exist in Taiwan and Korea. While these have not yet been markedly affected by the dynamics of resurgent nationalism, they well might. To glimpse a forerunner of this effect, one need only note how the nationalist policies of the Trump administration have affected the enrollment of international students in the United States. Reporting on the annual "Open Doors" survey of US higher education for 2018 indicates a decline in such enrollments for the second consecutive year, in this case amounting to a decline of 6.6% for the 2017–2018 academic year. In specific, new enrollments at the undergraduate level declined 6.3%, 5.5% at the graduate level, and 9.7% at the non-degree level (Redden 2018). Thus, as both national governments and individual HEIs continue to ramp up their recruitment of international students—for reasons ranging from the need to develop external funding to the desire to create "international" experiences for local students in their own countries—practitioners and policy makers alike are struggling with the tension between the unavoidable reality of globalization and the intense forces of nationalism, in their own countries and around the world.

The chapters in this volume, in many ways, offer a snapshot and an interpretation of the institutional, national, and regional efforts being pursued within the HE sector in this current interconnected political climate. While domestic issues and the needs of local communities are, on the one hand, important for HE to attend to, finding ways to harness the potential benefits (whatever they are understood to be) of an internationalized system, student body, and/or curriculum (among other markers of internationalization) are also priorities for many. Finding an appropriate integration between what many understand as opposites (but, we argue, should not be seen as such) is the challenge of the times. The authors featured in the preceding chapters indicate how this challenge is being met across the Asia Pacific region in contextually specific ways. Our intention is not to suggest that one or many approaches are gold standards or are even relevant to other contexts. Instead, we hope that what we have compiled here in this volume brings awareness to the efforts that are underway in the region and perhaps inspires further thinking about the possibilities and complexities of an internationalized HE sector.

While this volume is embedded in a specific historical and political moment, and, no doubt, the manifestations of internationalization and nationalism will continue their speedy evolutions, the future direction of policy, research, and practice related to this topic relies on shared understandings and critical discourse about what has happened in the past. To that end, we are confident that this volume will contribute to the ongoing discussion among the actors of the international HE sector about how to adapt to the changing times while remaining committed to their local communities. How do we broaden our horizons and also stay true to ourselves? How do we share our own knowledge and also be open enough to recognize when we need to learn from others? How do we encourage others to leave their homes to join our communities and be bold enough to embrace their differences? There are no simple or enduring answers to these questions. Yet, as we attempt to find our way in this increasingly globalized world, we share our experiences and observations in hopes that others will do the same. In that way, we can, ideally, move forward with our work more informed, inspired, and committed.

REFERENCES

Hohmann, James, and Joanie Greve. 2019. Davos Is in Decline As Elite's Fail to Tackle the Globe's Biggest Problems. *Washington Post*, January 22.

Phillips, Matt. 2019. Stocks in U-Turn All But Erasing Losses Last Year. *The New York Times*, January 20, p. 1.

Redden, Elizabeth. 2018. New International Enrollments Decline Again. *Inside Higher Education*, November 13. Available at https://www.insidehighered.com/news/2018/11/13/new-international-student-enrollments-continue-decline-us-universities. Accessed January 22, 2019.

Tan, Huieing. 2019. China's Economy Grew 6.6% in 2018, the Lowest Pace in 28 Years. *CNBC*. Available at https://www.cnbc.com/2019/01/21/china-2018-gdp-china-reports-economic-growth-for-fourth-quarter-year.html. Accessed January 21, 2019.

INDEX

© The Editor(s) (if applicable) and The Author(s), under exclusive
license to Springer Nature Switzerland AG 2019
D. E. Neubauer et al. (eds.), *Contesting Globalization
and Internationalization of Higher Education*,
International and Development Education,
https://doi.org/10.1007/978-3-030-26230-3